TRINITY:
'43-'45

A Legacy for Life

GORDON PARRY

For Lyn and Paul with much affection and with happy recollections of times shared.

Gordon

Trinity College, Carmarthen Publications

9th August, 2002

Published by
Trinity College
Carmarthen

ISBN 0 9523755 16

Printed in Wales by
Dinefwr Press
Rawlings Road, Llandybïe
Carmarthenshire, SA18 3YD

These random recollections are dedicated
to Mam, to Dad;
to Hilda, to Bryn and to Mary;
and particularly to Glenys and to Catherine;
with respect for past and present and future
students of Trinity
and for all good teachers, everywhere

Contents

Foreword

BY THE PRINCIPAL OF TRINITY COLLEGE, CARMARTHEN

As Trinity College nears its 150th anniversary, thoughts turn naturally to the past as well as to the future, and there is no-one of greater eminence than Lord Parry to engage in lively reminiscence about his student days in college.

His account of his years at Trinity in the closing phase of the second world war has all the stamp of vitality and exuberance which have characterised the life of this remarkable man of Pembrokeshire.

At one level, it is extraordinarily entertaining, rich in detail and studded with humorous anecdotal recollection. It is brimful of warmth and affection, but never in the slightest degree patronising or ponderous. It carries the reader along with the kind of zest and energy which are typical of a man who has achieved not only a high position in State and nation but also has gained an immense measure of regard and popularity in the community to which he belongs with such evident pride.

However, the book's special quality is that the affectionate, often hilarious, events of Lord Parry's studentship at Trinity are set within the wider context of the worrying and wearying days of war-time sacrifice and suffering, so that the narrative becomes a commentary not only on the robust if somewhat restricted experience of student life but on his coming to terms with the realities of a troubled, conflict-ridden wider world.

There is a measured resonance about Lord Parry's response to his Trinity experience. "Fifty years ago", he writes, "I 'went up' to Trinity. In a sense, I've never 'gone down'." He writes without pomp or pomposity, and what comes through his lively, engaging account of his years in college is a sense of deep appreciation concerning the ways in which his life was moulded by the happenings, great and small, and, even more importantly, the relationships, which studded his student days.

Lord Parry reminds us that, in the fifty years since leaving Trinity, he has seen the wonders and the blunders, the beauties and the ugliness, of the world. He has led an almost uniquely full and fascinating life, and he has yet to write a greater book, in which he will evaluate the events and personalities of the complex and absorbing international mosaic of his time. His full biography, when it is published, will be a work of rivetting interest and will make an important contribution to evaluating our life and times from a thoughtfully rounded and highly individual perspective.

In the meantime, we are grateful to him for this enthusiastic response to the challenge of recalling the formative years of his childhood, youth and early manhood against the background of college and community with which so many of his readers will be familiar.

A meeting with Lord Parry is always a perfect antidote to any tendency to feeling jaded or discouraged. This gripping narrative will have the same beneficial effect for those who meet him only, or additionally, through the printed page.

There could be no brighter or livelier approach to the 150th anniversary of Wales's second oldest institution of higher education than to visit the college through the vivid recollections and sharp observations of one of Trinity's most illustrious former students, now an Honorary Fellow of the college and one of its most dedicated supporters.

A Life Peer since 1975, a former Chairman of the Wales Tourist Board, and a Deputy Lieutenant of the County of Dyfed, Lord Parry is a man of outstanding wisdom and experience in many fields, including the arts, tourism and broadcasting. He has travelled extensively as a lecturer in Europe, America and Australasia. We are proud to claim that his roots are planted firmly not only in his native Pembrokeshire but in the cloistered and cherished setting of Trinity College.

Clive Jones-Davies

Prologue

This book of mine is not the first to have been written about Trinity College, Carmarthen. It is unlikely to be the last. Looking back, through the rosy tints of retrospect, to the warm days of youth is one of the comforts of cold age.

"I am not, Dear Boy" – said that great son of Llanelli, Lord Elwyn-Jones, to me, once – "into my dotage, I'm happy to say ... but I've been into my anecdotage for years!" So have I, and I'm happy to say that, too.

Indeed, some lunch-table anecdotes about the Trinity College of the early 1940s and my days in residence as a wartime student, on borrowed time from conscription to military service – well received by present-day staff, and coinciding with the College's setting-up of its own book publishing committee – brought the suggestion that I should "write a book about it", and here it is!

Begun in the high summer of 1995; hand-written into several drafts by the autumn; photo-copied for reading by Principal Clive Jones-Davies; read, re-read, sub-edited and tactfully bowdlerized – to save the blushes of the innocent! – by veteran author and College lecturer-emeritus, Gareth Hughes; amended, addended and, here and there, corrected, by life-long friend and school and College contemporary Cecil Parry, who shared our Trinity stage throughout with Eric Orsman, Barry Owen, David Oliver and Alan Stanford, the outside-augmented "Pembrokeshire Gang"; it reached the desk of the Principal's secretary, Mrs Sylvia Jones, and the word processor of Mrs Ann Evans, before Christmas.

There were never safer hands than theirs with a manuscript. There were never fewer grumbles, as additions, in scrawled writing, appeared on pristine pages, over and over again. It wasn't simply professionalism, which one takes for granted at such a level, but a creative involvement in this book.

I need to thank, too, a "senior" of mine, Tom Buckthought, for help and guidance; the "survivor" Jim Davies, for heroically surviving to write "A Leap in the Dark" and for giving me permission to quote from it, and, of course, for 50 years of his friendship.

Desmond and Silvia Davies read a pre-print copy, even though Desmond – a former Trinity student – was deep into the production of his comprehensive history of the Neyland in which his family and mine have grown. Simon Hancock heard me read early drafts of chapters, and Robert Reeves read my prose and his poetry aloud to me.

Vicky Riddle, my own secretary, has heard or read every word of almost every draft, checking and researching facts for me, despite heavy commitments of work elsewhere.

And then there was Glenys, my wife, and there was Catherine, our daughter, who were pursued from time to time, by me, with my sheets of paper, and lost me to my subterranean study for days and weeks on end. Catherine's approval of what she had read – "especially the bits about Neyland" – was particularly good for me, and Glenys, even after half-a-century of my anecdotage, was patient as she heard it all over again.

Vernon Davies, Gordon John, David Evans and Derek Rees read and approved; Tina Charles, of the Carmarthen Heritage Centre, Chris Miller and Dewi Jones (Chairman) of the Gwili Railway Preservation Society, and Phil Howells, were willing with information, too.

John Harry, of the Neyland Community Education Centre and his staff there, helped with emergency photocopying.

Towards the end of these memories of mine – if you read them to the end – you'll find a melancholy quote from Benjamin Disraeli who, when he wrote "Coningsby", seemed jaundiced about life and had his character describe youth, manhood and old age as burdensome. That surprised me. My own regret is that tomorrow morning I shall not be carrying my fibre-case down Neyland Hill to Neyland Station to board a steam train and to go "up the line" to Trinity College, Carmarthen – the "first staging-post along the way" for me on an incredible journey that's taken me here, there and everywhere, these last fifty years. I would love to have another fifty as exciting ahead of me, and I wish those who do as much joy in them as the seven decades of my living have brought me.

Finally, I give thanks again to the long-dead Samuel and Mrs. Samuel Davies whose gift to my parents became, for me, a legacy for life.

Gordon Parry
August 1996

An Earlier View

Michael Gareth Llewellyn wrote in his book "Sand in the Glass" – thinly disguising Trinity, for some reason, as Tretowyn – of his days as a student. Many of his memories and lasting impressions match mine. His tribute to the College of the early inter-war years is worth quoting.

"I began to see what was at the back of this teaching business. I felt I might like it, after all. I saw the constructional side of teaching in the development of character and the growth of knowledge and power. I saw how society could not exist without education. Perhaps I could be an engineer, after all, in the sense of planning to teach people to live the good life, the happy life, the useful life. I began to feel that a teacher could be the architect of fate."

I am grateful to him, too, for these verses from a poem, "The Teacher", by Humbert Wolfe.

I also build, but not with steel nor stone,
but with the shadowy bricks of innocence
and mortar that the heart has made her own,
and what I build has neither roof nor fence
that can deflect
with limits or an end, the visionary architect.

This is more than the upward anguish of the spire,
more than the vaulting bridge, that all but flies:
it is the consecration and the fire.
Fallen from far; it is the voice that cries,
"Make the way smooth
for the feet of the Lord of the world whose name is youth."

Gordon Parry

CHAPTER ONE

The Legacy

When Samuel Davies died, almost no-one outside of Neyland would have noticed, but his dying opened up the world for me.

The man had been a coal-factor. Neyland was a rail terminus, and the railway was its lifeline. Isambard Kingdom Brunel – the little giant of the age of steam – had designed its station, its locomotive-holding depot and freight marshalling yards, to serve an Irish Sea and, more optimistically, the Atlantic Ocean ferry traffic.

Coal was at the heart of his optimism. Thousands and thousands of tons of it would be burned, banking steam for his paddle-wheeled leviathan liners and the express trains that would link them with London.

Isambard and his dream of trans-Atlantic ferrying were dead before Samuel was born but, as did Neyland itself, our man prospered on the optimism that outlived the dream and the dreamer. Samuel Davies factored coal, buying anthracite from Hook, Lawrenny, Saundersfoot and Ammanford and steam coal from the South Wales valleys, and selling it on. The coal "stage" at Neyland was a busy one.

As what were, eventually, the Great Western Railway Company's trains steamed into the old market towns and little-known villages west of Cardiff, their rail-heads became trading distribution centres. They prospered, too, over the next fifty years.

At the end of the line, and at the beginning of this century, with freight, cattle and passengers in and out of Ireland, to and from the Cleddau estuary, Samuel Davies made money factoring coal. Samuel David Gordon Parry was to benefit.

When I was three-years-old, in 1929, my father, Thomas Lewis Parry, had become the pastor of Bethesda Baptist Church, Neyland, moving into the large, red-brick, post-Evan Roberts Revival, chapel in the High Street to minister to a congregation in which railwaymen and their families were prominent. Neither Samuel Davies nor his wife was a member there.

Samuel was a Calvinistic Methodist. He went marching to Zion, further along the High Street. Mrs. Samuel Davies – who seemed content to bury her own Christian name in her husband's – was a Salvationist. She wore the uniform of General William Booth's Christian Army when appropriate. She played a spirited accordion, when appropriate or not.

My father's sermons were evangelical. His pulpit presence was persuasive; his pastoral visiting persistent. "It's easier to go to chapel every Sunday than to find an excuse for Mr. Parry when he taps the door on Monday", the Bethesda Baptists said. Mrs. Samuel Davies was recruited. The Davieses and the Parrys – who were ten years younger than they were – became friends.

A County Councillor, Chairman of Pembrokeshire's Education Committee, Poor Law Guardian, school governor – all roles in which Dad would eventually follow him – and a Justice of the Peace, publicly involved, personally quiet, Mr. Davies shared with his wife an acute intelligence. Childless, they – especially she – were interested in the education of other people's children.

To take tea at their home in the 'thirties was to climb the social ladder. On the corner, where Lawrenny Street runs down into High Street, their house was large enough to accommodate the Neyland branch of Lloyds Bank as well as Mr. and Mrs. Davies and their elegant Victoriana.

"Would you like to see the Bank?" Samuel Davies would ask. It was a visitor's treat to tour the Bank. Not too many people had a Bank in their front room and there was still enough innocence left in our world then for the landlord to hold a key and to have right of access – "in case of emergency" – to the premises, after hours. So we would stand in the unlocked doorway and stare at the polished redwood counter that smelled of beeswax and shone from "elbow grease"; at the safety grille that beamed and breathed "Brasso"; and at the back-to-front LLOYDS BANK, gilded by Dickie Hughes on to the smoked plate-glass of the barred and bolted street door and frosted window. Seeing the Bank was always a prelude to taking tea. "There's lovely!" my mother would say, to both tour and tea-table.

We, the Parrys, lived in a terraced house. 15 John Street was not the only manse in the street. The Methodists had one there,

CHAPTER ONE

The Legacy

When Samuel Davies died, almost no-one outside of Neyland would have noticed, but his dying opened up the world for me.

The man had been a coal-factor. Neyland was a rail terminus, and the railway was its lifeline. Isambard Kingdom Brunel – the little giant of the age of steam – had designed its station, its locomotive-holding depot and freight marshalling yards, to serve an Irish Sea and, more optimistically, the Atlantic Ocean ferry traffic.

Coal was at the heart of his optimism. Thousands and thousands of tons of it would be burned, banking steam for his paddle-wheeled leviathan liners and the express trains that would link them with London.

Isambard and his dream of trans-Atlantic ferrying were dead before Samuel was born but, as did Neyland itself, our man prospered on the optimism that outlived the dream and the dreamer. Samuel Davies factored coal, buying anthracite from Hook, Lawrenny, Saundersfoot and Ammanford and steam coal from the South Wales valleys, and selling it on. The coal "stage" at Neyland was a busy one.

As what were, eventually, the Great Western Railway Company's trains steamed into the old market towns and little-known villages west of Cardiff, their rail-heads became trading distribution centres. They prospered, too, over the next fifty years.

At the end of the line, and at the beginning of this century, with freight, cattle and passengers in and out of Ireland, to and from the Cleddau estuary, Samuel Davies made money factoring coal. Samuel David Gordon Parry was to benefit.

When I was three-years-old, in 1929, my father, Thomas Lewis Parry, had become the pastor of Bethesda Baptist Church, Neyland, moving into the large, red-brick, post-Evan Roberts Revival, chapel in the High Street to minister to a congregation in which railwaymen and their families were prominent. Neither Samuel Davies nor his wife was a member there.

Samuel was a Calvinistic Methodist. He went marching to Zion, further along the High Street. Mrs. Samuel Davies – who seemed content to bury her own Christian name in her husband's – was a Salvationist. She wore the uniform of General William Booth's Christian Army when appropriate. She played a spirited accordion, when appropriate or not.

My father's sermons were evangelical. His pulpit presence was persuasive; his pastoral visiting persistent. "It's easier to go to chapel every Sunday than to find an excuse for Mr. Parry when he taps the door on Monday", the Bethesda Baptists said. Mrs. Samuel Davies was recruited. The Davieses and the Parrys – who were ten years younger than they were – became friends.

A County Councillor, Chairman of Pembrokeshire's Education Committee, Poor Law Guardian, school governor – all roles in which Dad would eventually follow him – and a Justice of the Peace, publicly involved, personally quiet, Mr. Davies shared with his wife an acute intelligence. Childless, they – especially she – were interested in the education of other people's children.

To take tea at their home in the 'thirties was to climb the social ladder. On the corner, where Lawrenny Street runs down into High Street, their house was large enough to accommodate the Neyland branch of Lloyds Bank as well as Mr. and Mrs. Davies and their elegant Victoriana.

"Would you like to see the Bank?" Samuel Davies would ask. It was a visitor's treat to tour the Bank. Not too many people had a Bank in their front room and there was still enough innocence left in our world then for the landlord to hold a key and to have right of access – "in case of emergency" – to the premises, after hours. So we would stand in the unlocked doorway and stare at the polished redwood counter that smelled of beeswax and shone from "elbow grease"; at the safety grille that beamed and breathed "Brasso"; and at the back-to-front KNAB SDYOLL, gilded by Dickie Hughes on to the smoked plate-glass of the barred and bolted street door and frosted window. Seeing the Bank was always a prelude to taking tea. "There's lovely!" my mother would say, to both tour and tea-table.

We, the Parrys, lived in a terraced house. 15 John Street was not the only manse in the street. The Methodists had one there, as well as the Baptists. Theirs was at 53, on the same side of the street and in the same style as ours. They were straight-forward places with a front room, a middle room, a back kitchen and a lean-to scullery. I've learned since that size, scale, area and difference in living space define – even determine – social dimension. The Davieses' house was different.

Connected to and, normally locked off from, the Bank was – to my boy's eye – a cavern of a room. Not so much lit as shadowed by one, narrow, out-of-scale sash-window in the eastern wall, its floor ran on – through the thrown shadows – raising itself, mid-way, up several steps, to split a dining-area level from the sitting-space. There was a further lift of steps to a grained door that – standing shut – concealed the stairs to the bedrooms above. Years later, I saw Samuel Davies "laid out" in the largest of them: lying in scale as well as in state. At the back of the downstairs cavern, beyond the fireplace, there were French doors that opened on to a glassed-in, backyard conservatory that was called "the green house". There was even another house, integral to the main house, on its Lawrenny Street frontage. Miss Nellie Roach lived there with her widowed mother. Miss Roach was housemaid to the Davieses and cleaner of Lloyds Bank.

Tea was always set on a round table in that thin window of the dining area. My mother had been "in good service" as a sempstress – never to be spelled by her as the common "seamstress" – and she set a fine table herself. Bone china, crotcheted lace cloths and Colmans-starched linen, "covered" with electroplated, nickel-silver cutlery and whitest of white serviettes, welcomed the many visitors to Bethesda Manse. Preachers and their wives from across Wales praised Mam's Maids of Honour, her Navvy's Wedding Cake and whole-hearted hospitality; so it wasn't the artifacts, nor even the knowledge that the Davieses' silver was hall-marked and "solid", that distinguished their teas from ours. It was the wealth of shop-bought confectionery!

Brought up on home-made delights, however deft and delicious, at the prospect of three-tiered cake-stands piled high with Kup-Kakes, more than one Scribona roll, sliced in thick cutlets, with all the lumpy chocolate-coated ends waiting to be claimed, and "individual", fresh-fruit pies, straight from their colourful cardboard boxes, surrounded by iced-slices, oozing custard and, on a central silver dish, a mini-mountain of Mock Macaroons, a schoolboy would have been a saint not to drool. I drooled.

There was another mountain of wonder there. It was on the window-sill. In a perfect sphere – a ball of glass, set on ebony legs and clawed feet – was a miniature mountain village in Switzerland. I was allowed to pick up that small world and to turn it over. When I did, and reversed it again, a blizzard blew out of nowhere and the chalets were lost in snow-flakes that, in a moment or two, thinned themselves out and settled, one by tiny one, on the roofs, on the church steeple and on the mountains, drifting into the lakes and river valleys. I'd been born in a blizzard. One of the very few blizzards to blow into Pembrokeshire as early as November had complicated my arrival at Molleston Manse, near Templeton, Narberth, on 30th November, 1925. Julius Caesar, St. Andrew, Winston Churchill and I all came in – some distance apart, in time and status – on the 30th of November. I haven't checked on St. Andrew or Sir Winston but Caesar had entered in a storm, as well as being "from his mother's womb untimely ripped".

It hadn't been quite so dramatic as that for Mam and for me but it hadn't been easy, either, and much too much for Miss Merriman, the amateur midwife.

"All that snow blowin' an' ewer Dad sent after the doctor from Narberth – both of them on horses ridin' back through the blizzard!" I was told, often, in the years that followed.

Perhaps the uncommon, common portents gave me some atavistic sense of power as I turned that toy glass world upside-down but it was the beauty born out of turning it to rights again that had me dazzled with delight – delusions of grandeur or not!

Nellie Roach was in and out of the greenhouse that doubled as a kitchen. Why they needed a kitchen when everything they ate seemed to come ready to eat in cardboard boxes intrigued me but not nearly so much as Nellie's progress around the room. The rotund lady had, my father told me, "lost" a leg. Careless, that seemed. "But", I said, "she still has two." "Yes, that's right. She has, but one's a cork leg now, artificial."

I'd known Miss Roach long enough – been in her company often enough – to come to terms with her idiosyncratic undercarriage. What I could never ignore was the loud squeak that came from it every time she moved her prosthesis, and the clump with which her false foot hit the floor, rattling the cups in their saucers on the table. My imitation of her perambulation

Anne Parry and son Gordon Parry at the doorway of Molleston Chapel, 1926.

became a very private family party-piece. Wiping tears of laughter away, my mother would say, "Shame on ewe. 'Ewe'll be stuck like that one day, my boy! Mockin' the afflicted!"

I was "stuck like that". Whether my imitation of Nellie or my even crueller copying of the lopsided gait of Freddie Philpin – a High Street green-grocer, high tenor and sermon-taster – had anything to do with it, I've limped heavily myself for thirty years, but that's another book, and this one isn't written yet.

Not perhaps an opinionated man but, certainly, a man of firm opinions, Samuel Davies was heard with respect in our house. He was quoted.

"Mr. Samuel Davies", my mother would say, "doesn't think that ministers' manses should be in streets. He thinks that ministers and their families should be detached – living in places with their own ground around them – like vicars. 'More dignity about it!' he says."

Both my mother and Mr. Samuel Davies were snobs: nice snobs but snobs nonetheless. In upwardly mobile and socially depressed Wales, "bettering" themselves had been a part of their Nonconformist ethic. Mrs. Samuel Davies was a snob, too. A helpful snob – every bit as nice as the other two – her templates were the Royal Family. She knew the names and relations, chances and mischances, legal and "morganatic" marriages, of anyone who'd ever shared a bloodline with Queen Victoria or a bed with John Brown. Expert in regal genealogy, her recitation of their love-lives, their couplings and connections, lit the shades of the cavern for my mother as Nellie Roach cleared the tea-things and I sat, hidden and momentarily forgotten, cwtched among chenille cloths and velvet curtains that smelled of camphor balls – with the glass heaven and earth in one hand and the squirrelled butt-end of a Scribona roll in the other – listening especially acutely when Mrs. Samuel Davies's voice dropped to a whisper and Mam said, "Possible?", or "Never!", or "Well! Whoever would have believed it?"

There was a time – two or three years later – when Mr. Samuel Davies's snobbish opinions put pressure on me. They stopped me working for Flossie Griffiths.

"D'you think it's right", he asked my mother, "a minister's son pushing a hand-cart around the town selling groceries?"

I was thirteen-years-old. Lilian Gwyther, Freddie "Guff" Griffiths and I worked together on Saturday mornings, in the run-up to the Second World War, wheeling Flossie's hand-cart around Belle View, Charles Street, James Street, Honeyborough Road, West Lane, Water Street and Honeyborough Green, selling groceries and sweets. We were building up the trade. The Munich Crisis had come and gone, but even we three knew that war wasn't far away. "Rationing", they said, would follow. Quite apart from all that, I knew where the Baptists lived. Where my Dad tapped, we tapped too. We were raising the take so substantially that Flossie raised our wages. She was paying me a whole half-crown every Saturday – at a time when my father was only getting four pounds for a full week at his calling – when Mr. Samuel Davies intervened.

This man was in trade himself. He never soiled his hands with the coal that other men cut and carried, but he bought and sold it at a profit. I never understood why he should trade and I shouldn't, but I was told to resign.

Neither Lilian, Freddie, Flossie nor I could believe it. Miss Flossie Griffiths was not very much more than four and a half feet tall. She was, though, full of life. Her shop had been designed to fit her, and she walked around its counters on platforms, with all the shelves low enough for her to reach. We loved that little lady. When I finished my final round, she gave me a ten-shilling note as a farewell bonus. I'd never owned one before. I held it for a little while – a minute or two – then I gave it back to her and bought from her a blue bowl, patterned with flowers, set on a silvered stand that could almost have been solid but was stamped E.P.N.S. The stand had a shining, chrome-steel nut-cracker hanging from it, and the bowl was full of elegant chocolates, interspaced with filberts, walnuts and Brazils. My mother couldn't speak when I took it home to her. She didn't even say, "There's lovely!" but I knew what she meant when she put her hand out and touched my face. Her face was flushed. Her eyes were clouded. There was silence between us. The silence was all that was necessary. There are times when those who love words love each other too much to need them.

Later, she said: "Perhaps it's for the best, Boy? If this ole war's comin', there'll be nothin' to sell from Flossie's cart, rationin' an' all. Another war! Possible if they'll let it happen, surely? Just as everything was comin' back into the shops lovely after the last ole war!"

When, four years later, Samuel Davies intervened again in my life, the war was on, rationing was in, the cart was redundant, and he was dead. I'd loved our "round", delighting in the selling and the banter on the doorsteps. "Guff" Griffiths and I were soul-mates, and Lilian was lovely. It's a good job the man did, posthumously, what he did or I never would have forgiven him. He'd been dead a fair while when we learned what he had done.

By then, I was 16-years-old and – after a fractured middle-schooling while the bombs, for a while, "blitzed" Pembroke Dock, and all but closed our County Intermediate School there – I was in the Lower Sixth. A number of our former classmates were not. They'd died, in the rubble of their homes, in the indiscriminate deadliness of a wartime West Wales night.

The rest of us had, temporarily, been taught in our home districts, scattered around village halls and Sunday School-rooms, for the months of the worst of the bombing and enemy mining of the estuary. We'd won our Central Welsh Board certificates on return to the Fifth Form and were coming to grips with Higher Certificate or Matriculation Exemption when a bomb of another sort burst amongst us.

H. M. Dowling, M.A., our headmaster, was an English teacher of genius, a poet of sorts, and moonlighted as a literary critic for the "Western Mail". He'd succeeded an authoritarian – Trevor Jones, M.A. – and quickly established a friendly relationship with the school at a difficult time. He was, it seems, not as fond of administration as he was of teaching. More than halfway through our first year to Higher examinations, he discovered that there were no longer university arts courses for physically fit male students old enough to be conscripted into the armed forces. He arrived amongst us during someone else's lesson. We were to be sent home, there and then, with letters of explanation to our parents. That meant a double trip across the Haven for me, from the Hobb's Point to the Neyland Pontoon and back.

I'm not even certain, now, whether my parents had thought my education through as far as university entrance. As I was the youngest of four, three of whom had flown the nest, they'd been able to keep me on at school longer than the others, who had all left when training for work "with prospects" had become available. Almost the whole of our 'twenties generation and all of the lads left in our Sixth Form were the first in the history of their families to have any prospect of going on to university education. Then there would be the matter of cost. My parents had cherished the hope that I, too, might become a minister, or a missionary with the Baptist Missionary Society. I quite liked the thought of being a latter-day William Carey. Sagittarians like to travel!

Mr. Dowling – acutely embarrassed at having missed the growing threat to the chances of those whose parents expected them to go on to university – had, he thought, discovered a possible alternative route for all of us. A degree course took a minimum three years. A teacher training college course then took two. Indeed, it took only five academic terms in wartime, and legislation already existed for time-served sailors, soldiers and airmen to be grant-aided to further study on demobilisation. His letter to our parents proposed that we should each apply for admission to training colleges. Assuming success, we could be certificated teachers going into the services and graduate, at state expense, on coming out. In fact, this turned out not to be the case, and those who had received a teacher-training grant were precluded from applying for an undergraduate grant later!

My parents were pleased, rather than annoyed, by Mr. Dowling's letter. They signed agreement to my application and to my completing forms for entry to Trinity College, Carmarthen – "the poor man's university" – for the next academic year. There was, however, still a problem for them. The fees for residence in Trinity, per academic year, were £75. Such sums didn't accumulate in our house. Dad, though, didn't hesitate. "Where God guideth, He provideth" was one of his texts. "We'll manage", he said.

Back at school, later in the day, I discovered that I needed two referees to my character and suitability for teaching. Not feeling particularly God-guided, I might have had to go home again, across the Cleddau, to find them.

My father was Chairman of the School governors. One of his most active chapel members, Mrs. Norah Davies, B.A., also from John Street, Neyland, was a governor, too. Her home was on the telephone. Mr. Dowling arranged for her – she'd known me since I was three-years-old – to supply one reference. My formmate and namesake, but no relation, Cecil Parry, came up with a suggestion for the other referee.

"I'm going over to the vicarage now", he said. "Our vicar's doing a reference for me. I'm sure he'll do one for you." It was good that he was sure, because I wasn't. Ecumenism hadn't broken out then, not in Neyland anyway, and I was aware of a sort of armed truce between Baptists and Anglicans. Some of our pulpit preachers called vicars "Episcopalian priests" which, whatever it meant to them, seemed a bit strong to me. But Trinity College, Carmarthen, was a Church foundation and, since Cecil Parry, who attended Bethel Baptist Chapel in Pembroke Dock, had told me, in confidence, that he thought he was agnostic, if not atheist, and was, anyway, going to collect a reference from the Vicar, I went with him.

The Rev. Vernon Bartlett was very kind and very amused when I followed Cecil into his study. "Two Parrys for the price of one!" he exclaimed. "It's a good job that I know your Dad, young Parry from Neyland, because I don't know a thing about you."

That was exactly what the reference that he wrote for me said. He told the Principal, the Rev. Thomas Halliwell, with whom he was obviously friendly, that he was recommending me for entry to Trinity because of my father's qualities rather than my own. He added that my initiative – he might well have said my barefaced cheek – in asking him to be one of my referees probably showed that I could make progress.

The Rev. Vernon Bartlett, eventually, was to become Lord Bishop of St. Asaph so, that day, there were two Lords in Waiting in his vicarage study and neither of them would have dreamed it.

I have a copy of the letter written by Mrs. Norah Davies among my papers still. Helpful and supportive as the Vicar's, it contains one sentence that – as innocent then as the day was long – couldn't be written now. "I have known Gordon Parry since he was a child", she wrote, "and have long been intimate with the members of his family."

So strongly, if unusually, supported, my application was, in time, successful. So were those of Cecil Parry and Eric Orsman. Elmer Jenkins, John Powell and others, who were younger than we were, could afford to wait another year and were accepted for entry to St. Paul's College in Cheltenham in 1944, but the Lower Sixth, as we'd known it, was set to disintegrate. We had no need to take "Mock Higher" examinations too seriously after that. Some of us found paid work to help with buying all the equipment listed in the prospectus as vital to studying at college. With summer holidays near, I became a temporary clerk in the Pembrokeshire War Agricultural Executive's office in Barn Street,

Haverfordwest, where – the only male in a room full of married women whose husbands were away at the war – I quickly discovered how inadequate my education had been up to then and was teased unmercifully.

I was seventeen years and six months old, with the call-up age set at seventeen years and eight months, as that wartime summer of 1943 warmed up, and there was still the unresolved matter of a residential fee that equalled almost one-third of my father's annual salary.

It was at that moment – though he was dead – that Mr. Samuel Davies came back into my life. He didn't do so physically, of course. He was represented, "personated", by his widow and her housemaid.

We were finishing an evening meal in our kitchen-living-room when Mrs. Samuel Davies and Miss Nellie Roach came, squeaking and clumping, through the oil-clothed passage to join us there. Nellie carried an oblong parcel wrapped in the "Western Mail" and bound with twine. Neither of them made any reference to it when it was placed on a corner of the table. It simply rested there as fresh cups were set, tea poured, cake-tins opened, and conversation about anything but that parcel began.

Nothing was said about it, either, during the half-hour that followed but, on the Parry side, curiosity was mounting. Occasionally, eyes would wander to it. A family eyebrow would be raised, if family glances coincided. The parcel sat where it was, as supercilious as an inanimate object without eyebrows can be.

At last, the two ladies prepared to leave. Mrs. Davies got to her feet and Nellie to her foot, swaying until her cork leg kick-started her on to even keel. Then, and only then, did Mrs. Samuel Davies lay her hand on the print of the parcel.

"Now!" she said. "Now! Mr. Parry! Sam wanted you to have what's in here. You and Mrs. Parry have been so kind to us – were so kind to us all the time that Samuel was ill. He appreciated it so much and he left instructions that you were to be given what is in this parcel as a token of his appreciation, and that you were to have it as soon as it could be arranged."

The Salvation Army sense of theatre was reasserting itself. Mrs. Davies was enjoying herself. "But you mustn't open it yet!" She wagged a finger at my father.

"You mustn't open it, in fact, until Miss Roach and I have left John Street. Will you promise me that?"

Dad did, of course. John Street is a long street. It runs from west to east, perfectly level, for several hundred yards. It was going to be a longish postponement but my father said, "Very well, then. What a lovely mystery! We can't really thank you properly, can we? Until we know what we are thanking you for. However, Gordon can watch you until you turn the corner. I promise not to open the parcel till then."

Nellie Roach was enjoying herself, too. Goodbyes were said, with a giggle or two. We left the kitchen door and the passage glass-door open as I escorted them through the storm-door. As they took off, cheerfully, along the pavement, with a swing, a squeak and a clump, every yard of the way, I stood and watched and waited. Finally, they reached the corner of Frederick Street and, with a farewell flourish of Nellie's walking-stick, they were gone.

"Right!" I shouted. "You can undo it. They're out of sight!" as I doubled back to the kitchen.

Dad hadn't cheated. He hadn't lost any time, either. A farm-boy at heart, he always carried "a cutting knife" with the peppermints in his waistcoat pocket. The twine fell away from the parcel. The "Western Mail" went next.

Then, breath was held and there was a silence that went on so long that it became embarrassing. In fact, for a moment, all three of us were embarrassed.

"Will you look at that?" my father asked. It was a rhetorical question. Mam and I had been looking at "that" ever since the paper had come off it.

"That" was a bigger bundle of brand-new £1 notes than either one of us had ever seen or expected to see on our kitchen table.. Eventually, we counted one hundred of them: one hundred of the blue-into-pink £1 notes that had been designed, printed, and issued as a war-time emergency currency to foil Nazi counterfeiters, only a short while before.

"There you are", said Dad. "I said we'd manage. You are right for college now, Boy!"

My mother, unexpectedly subdued, counted the notes again. "Yes! It is!" she said, sounding close to tears. "It's one 'undred, exactly."

As I said a while ago, "When Samuel Davies died, almost no-one outside of Neyland would have noticed, but his dying opened up the world for me." In a little over a month, I would be catching a train – 3rd Class – out of Neyland Station to take up residence at Trinity College, Carmarthen.

As epic journeys go, the forty miles of travel to the next county don't amount to much when you think of any one of the missionaries that I might have been, but they were a beginning. There was a whole world to travel "up the line" – and Coleg y Drindod, Caerfyrddin, was my first staging-post along the way.

As legacies go, one hundred new pound-notes wrapped in an old newspaper don't sound too exciting, either, in the Lottery Land of 1996, but, half-a-century ago, they were the keys to doors that might have stayed locked for my lifetime. Even Flossie Griffiths might have forgiven Samuel Davies had she known. Lilian Gwyther and Freddie Griffiths never did, because they never knew.

CHAPTER TWO

The Line

You know, already, that the railway was Neyland's life-line. From our terminus town – whether by road or by rail – there was only one direction heading out of it. Anywhere beyond Honeyborough was "up the line". When we travelled further than that, we left our families and friends "down below".

"Excuse me, does this train stop at Neyland?" travellers – anxious in the "black-out" of the war – would ask Phil Phillips, the Guard.

"Oh! I do hope so, Boss", he'd tease. "If it doesn't, we're all goin' to get very wet!"

On a point of the north shore of the Cleddau, bounded to the east by Barn Lake Pill, to the south by the deep salt waters of the estuary, and with only thirty miles or so of land to the west between them and St. Brides Bay, Neyland people's sense of orientation was unique. Eastwards was upwards. That concept of geographic relationship was as old as our history, pre-dating Brunel and his railway by eight hundred years and more.

Pembrokeshire – a peninsula thrusting further westward into the sea than any in Britain, save that other Land's End in Cornwall – had sub-divided itself early into two cultures, the one, indigenous, the other, incoming and alien. "Pembroke" was what the invaders made of "Pen-fro", which, in the old tongue – "yr hen iaith" – meant Head-land or Land's-end.

Almost all those invaders of Britain had come, eventually, to the western end of its mainland. Some came directly and on purpose. Some, blown off course, were lucky to arrive at all, by accident. Others came the long way round, via "the Marches".

Most of the influences – linguistic, cultural, political, religious and denominational – that shaped the English, wherever they lived, and the English language, as spoken in England, found a foothold on the accessible easy terrain, with its contours hardly ever rising above the 200 feet of the plateau, between Pembrokeshire's southern sea-coast and the Cleddau.

North of the Haven, say the early maps, was "the Welsherie", south of it, "the Englisherie", and there was a line of division drawn – on vellum and on the ground – between them. There was a name for that line, neither a Welsh nor an English name, but one borrowed from earlier invaders, probably the Norsemen. That dividing line was "the Landsker" and behind it ran the Preseli range, the natural redoubt and bastion of the Cymru.

Reinforced by the invaders – crenellated with a chain of castles from St. Davids, on St. Bride's Bay, to Laugharne, on Carmarthen Bay – the Landsker "drew the line" from beyond which "y fro Cymraeg" could not be dislodged by "les étrangers", the Norman and other "strangers". To this day, this line is still traced on the ground and in the hearts, the minds, the spirits – and in the languages, the accents, the dialects, of "up the line" and of "down below" Pembrokeshire.

At some distant point in its history, an order of monks set up their monastery on what became known as Gellyswick, between Milford town and the Dale Roads. Because they had crossed Wales from England, they named their enclave "Anglia trans-Walia", in Roman Catholic, Latin tradition. Out of that nostalgic name came "Little England Beyond Wales", so incorrectly applied by so many for so long to the whole of Pembrokeshire, ignoring the fact that, above the line, the Welsh language lives – rich, idiosyncratic, evocative – matching, in its lovely, archaic individuality, the English still spoken by the people within the pale of south Pembrokeshire, where Chaucerian and Shakespearian syntax and Norman French nouns and pronouns, in my childhood, enriched the accent and the dialect almost into patois.

It was a "down-below" boy in his eighteenth year who, on 2nd September, 1943, carried his bulging, weighty fibre case along John Street, down Frederick Street into the High Street – passing Lloyds Bank and watched from its doorstep, waved on his way, by Mrs. Samuel Davies and Miss Nellie Roach – descending the 1-in-5 slope of the Neyland Hill; levelling out on to the cobbles in front of the Great Western Hotel, with its Brunel Hall; lifting the case through the "kissing gate" into the Hotel Gardens and came, finally, into Neyland Station that had, for so long, after the dream of its creator died – as Dylan said of Swansea's – "been above its station". Until only recently, when war broke out, it had had crystal-glass roofing to match, on a smaller scale, that of Paddington. Roofless, now, it still boasted 1st and 2nd Class waiting-rooms, "UP" and "DOWN" platforms, coal-gas lanterns and scrolled, cast-iron benches, fretted "G.W.R." There were, still, slim corinthian cast-pillars in chocolate and cream livery, left, supporting the air, at points along the platform.

All my senses are alert again to that September morning, half a century ago. I touch, I taste, I hear, I see, I smell the railway in its heyday of steam. I trace "T.C.C.", for Trinity College, Carmarthen, in the dust that, everywhere, defies the carriage cleaners. There is the carbon taste of coal-grit blowing on the wind. I look and look and look again along the length of the linked train of coaches and, beyond, to the pulsating impatience of the giant engine. Acrid hot smells – steam, soot, oil and boiler-water – condense and tingle as, breathed across the membranes at the back of my nose, they tease a sneeze. Above all, I sense the pent-up power of the moment – the kinetic energy held in control – waiting to move mountains and me and my fibre case to Trinity College, Carmarthen. I know what it feels like to go to the moon.

"Bless you!" says my father, because I hadn't walked away from home alone. No-one ever did go to the station unescorted from our house, and anyone arriving at the station to stay with us was met there. Nor was walking the thousand yards, to or from John Street, hand-bagging cases, remarkable. There were only three cars in the whole street, and few enough in the town. What's more, petrol was rationed, and Greens' splendid "double-deckers" ran only along the Promenade, High Street and Kensington Road. Walking was taken for granted then. I'd sneezed, so "Bless you!" says my father.

It wasn't every day a man's son went off to be a student. It wasn't, in fact, so very long since Dad had been a student himself. In a back-street Chapel "Bible School" in Porth, in the Rhondda, a 29-year-old ex-coalminer and father of three children, he had studied, with other potential pastors, in the makeshift academy that the Rev. R. B. Jones and colleagues created to give some intellectual weight to the zeal and conviction of men and women, inspired beyond their own learning by the charisma and dynamism of Evan Roberts' spiritual Revival services in 1904-5.

My father and I were not alone on the platform. Some of his deacons were gathering. Dan James, the driver of the train, was my Sunday School teacher. Phil Phillips wasn't guarding the train that I was boarding but he'd come, from the other platform, to see me off. Mr. Jones, the Station Master, was there, too, with a friendly word. One or other of them put my heavy bag aboard. It was nearly time to go.

"Best climb in", said the Station Master. "He'll be whistling you out soon."

I'd been on much longer train journeys – to Gloucester, even – but this one topped them all for excitement.

It's difficult to remember, now, the difference between Third and Second Class rail travel, other than the smaller cost of it, but Third Class there was and Third Class I travelled, in a non-corridor coach, with a netted rack overhead for luggage, and neat, little, glass globes to throw light on framed prints of places with names that I'd never heard and could scarcely pronounce.

The logo "G.W.R." was everywhere, woven into the carpets, frosted into the carriage mirrors, branded into the woodwork of removable parts. Parts that moved, unofficially, and reappeared, still branded, as adornments to Neyland homes, were said to have been gifted to them by that mysterious, communal benefactor, George William Rees. "See? It has his initials on it."

Dan James, a humorous, robust man, about to leave for the footplate, said: "I'll tell you the difference between classes, Gordon. On steep hills, First Class passengers remain seated. Second Class passengers get out and walk. Third Class passengers get out and push." The joke was as old as the stage-coach but it won a great laugh.

Nowadays, small children fly the Atlantic in the care of cabin-crews with less attention paid to their leaving than my family and our friends gave to mine. My father had, publicly, kissed me goodbye. That could have embarrassed but didn't, nor did it surprise me. We were a demonstrative lot, we Parrys. We kissed each other goodnight and good morning. There was nothing "sissy" about that Radnorshire man kissing his adolescent Pembrokeshire son who was leaving home, even though he was only going to Carmarthen.

All the carriage windows were blanked with green netting, designed to save the passengers from splintering glass if the train was bombed in transit. My carriage window had been lowered on its heavy leather strap. The group on the platform was, hugely, off-level with me but every member of it lined up and reached up to shake my hand, in final farewell, through the open window.

Given that hundreds had gone off to the war in the last four years from Neyland station and that Clemmie Mathias was already dead as a result of it, perhaps my own leaving was overstated, but I didn't notice it at the time.

A heavy signal-arm crashed to green. The Guard's flag matched it in colour and movement. His Acme "Thunderer" thundered its warbling whistle. The chains linking the rolling-stock clanked taut – slackened – tautened – as the wheels gripped and slipped on the shining steel of the tracks. The engine was taking the strain of the train and we began, slowly, to move away.

"Goodbye, Dad!" I shouted. "See you at Half Term!"

My father nodded. His Anthony Eden hat was doffed. He'd begun to go bald in his early twenties and, since then, he'd combed a wing of his red hair up and over his poll. As he waved his hat, the wing flew free, standing upright – waving to me, too! – as the train gathered speed. The fireman, on the footplate, took the "Pass" from the signal-man at the signal-box window, hooking an arm through the metal loop and taking the key in-board. Then, the bulk of the engine-shed blocked my view of the platform. In moments, we were under Darky's Bridge, past the Gas works, past the gasometer, and running free. I could have sat down then, but I didn't.

Back at home, my mother – who had said her goodbyes after breakfast – would be tidying the nest from which the last of her brood had just flown, free as his father's wing of hair.

Instead of sitting down, I crossed the carriage. The tide was high in the Pill. The salt-water covered the Stepping Stones, and the trees of the woods along the bank washed their lower branches in it. Swans paddled there, unmoved in their majesty by the rattling and the rumbling on the railway. Mallard and moor-hen seemed fussier – rising briefly from, then falling back on to, the surface, as the backwater narrowed under the foot-bridge at Westfield crossing and the line took to the fields as it skirted Rosemarket.

The valley was as green as Richard Llewellyn's ever was and I'd caught minnows and tickled small trout in the leafy river under the Upper Crossing wall. While Europe tore itself apart and tracer bullets, bombs, land-mines, sea-mines and oil-tank fires had brought the war home to the shores of the Cleddau – where squadrons of seaplanes rode the water, racing from it into the sky to police and protect the convoys, gathering in the

Haven before braving the Western Approaches – our childhood had been free and easy. Even after air-raids – on the All Clear – we'd searched for shrapnel; for the fins of incendiary bombs whose white fire had burned out, harmlessly, in the turf; and for silks and cords from mine parachutes in the broken trees around the craters that they'd blown. Perhaps – in all that warring – we had been the last generation to be free, to be at peace with ourselves, wandering – without fear of "funny" people – far from home and delighting in discovering Pembrokeshire, below and along its lines.

I crossed and recrossed that carriage as it clickety-clacked, clickety-clacked, clickety-clacked, to and beyond Johnston until we moved into less familiar territory – entering, stopping at, and leaving Haverfordwest. I took my seat at Clarbeston Road and still had the carriage to myself at Clunderwen.

Ronnie Lawrence, Cecil Parry and Eric Orsman had planned to join me at Whitland, and I think that it was probably at the border town station that I first had sight of Barry Owen from Narberth. Whitland was the junction where trains from south of the river rendezvoused with the main Pembrokeshire to Paddington line out of Neyland.

The carriage had cooled as I moved from open window to open window. I closed both of them, hauling on the straps. On the safety net there was an official sticker. On the sticker was a cartoon. It featured Mr. Chad, a creation of the Ministry of Information, peeping over a blind at a rail passenger who was peeling back the green net from a window so as to see out. Mr. Chad was admonishing the traveller in a rhyming couplet.

The couplet said: "Pardon me for my correction,
That stuff is there for your protection.

In the free space underneath a better wit, as good a poet, had added his own lines.

Thank you for the information,
But I can't see the bloody station!"

I sympathised, totally. With the window shut, I could see nothing. As I dropped it again, the train steamed into Whitland Station and there were the friends with whom I was to spend a great deal of time over the next two years. The lads from down below were only one station away from Carmarthen and their initiation at Trinity College. Their lives would never be the same again.

King Alfred's and Trinity Colleges, 1943-44.

CHAPTER THREE

The Initiation

As we off-loaded our luggage on the platform at Carmarthen – still high on our own local and particular excitement as form-mates and friends moving further afield together – we realised that we were by no means the only new students to have arrived. Other trains had brought other "freshmen". They were already gathered under the station's clock, more or less organised into a group, and exchanging introductions. Ronnie Lawrence, a "senior" now, having gone up to Trinity in 1942 from our school, effected ours.

The first surprise was the age-range of that group. Some of the men in it looked old enough – it transpired that they were old enough – to be the fathers of some of the others.

Barry Owen was even younger than the three of us from our school. He looked it, too. E. Barry Owen, whose father was a teacher at the Narberth Primary School, turned out to be bright beyond his years, with a C.W.B. matriculation and Higher Certificate exemption already behind him. He was a soccer player of some skill and – even more to be admired – not only played jazz cornet but had his cornet with him.

John Rees, on the other hand, a grown man who had come from up-the-line to join the platform gathering, was well into his thirties, and looked more.

He and some of our future colleagues at the then all-male college had been away to the war and come back. Some had been invalided out of service. There was even talk that day of one – aptly named Noble – having been an exchanged prisoner-of-war. Certainly, John Rees, a pre-war, uncertificated teacher, had been a non-commissioned officer, seen service overseas, and was, now, a prospective re-entrant to the classroom – as a student, first, and, with luck, eventually, – as a certificated teacher.

The age-range, interesting though it was, didn't seem to

matter just then. All of us were excited and insecure. Perhaps the ex-servicemen were quieter. They'd joined other groups on other stations much further from home than any of us were now. They'd had authority over larger groups themselves. Perhaps because they had, they kept quiet. It was a services principle to volunteer nothing and to volunteer for nothing. The younger we were, the noisier we were.

Richard Fry's voice cut through the noise. We hadn't seen him approach us. Tall, good-looking, sure of himself, as public schoolboys tended to be then, he took charge.

"Welcome, gentlemen", he said. "Welcome to Carmarthen and to Trinity College. My name is Richard Fry. I am the General Prefect and Head of the Students' Council. You'll be glad to know that I have a bus outside, waiting to take you all to Trinity."

It was a revealing little speech. The young Englishman had called us all "gentlemen". It was a form of address that would become familiar but sounded like a promotion in status for we lads who were straight out of Sixth Form. Nor did I see anything wrong in a college having a Prefect. Most of us had been prefects in our schools. It must have sounded incongruous, though, for men nudging forty-years-old who had been off about the world defending democracy.

The fact was that Trinity College, Carmarthen, was, in 1943, being run as though its students were still at school. Its General Prefect was the Head Boy. The Students' Council was an extension of the College establishment. The democracy that some of those arriving with us had been fighting to preserve hadn't even reached Trinity! There were to be interesting times ahead in the cloistered corridors of college power, but no conflict yet. We picked up our bags and followed the "G.P."

If we'd forgotten that there was a war on, the bus reminded us. It was a "utility" vehicle. Basic in lay-out, efficient in petrol consumption, its seats were modelled on park-benches. Slatted wood on metal frames welcomed us. No-one grumbled. We were the "utility" generation. Had we grumbled, someone would have reminded us – "There's a war on, you know! There's worse than this in the trenches!"

We wore utility suits – pocketless, turn-up-less, almost seamless. We sat in utility furniture. It was inevitable that we should ride in a utility bus. They must have cut down on its springs, too, and, with the weight of bodies and of baggage, it felt as though our backsides occasionally dragged on the ground as we crossed the Tywi Bridge and turned below the ruins of Carmarthen Castle, heading for Lammas Street and the centre of town.

As we passed the Boar's Head Hotel, someone shouted, "There's the Whore's Bed!" It was an early introduction to a ribaldry – a particular humour, irreverent, out of context and very funny – that was to become part of life for me, not just for the next two years but for as long as I've lived.

Born to the manse, planned for the pulpit, bearing the burden early, in a cosmopolitan railway town of being "Parry, the Preacher's boy", I'd had to fight my corner in the back-lanes. I'd had to prove that I was as tough as the rest of our gang; climbing higher, diving deeper, swearing louder. I'd broken bones falling out of trees to prove my worth. We'd scrumped apples and "acquired" other things to which we had no right.

Fortunately, juvenile delinquency hadn't really been invented then. Happily, Police Sergeant James – a Calvinistic Methodist deacon, the choirmaster at Zion, and father of my good friend Trevor James – was content to be judge, jury and executioner of summary justice, corporal, physical, on the spot, and choosing the spot with skill.

It's said that when Leo Abse, the Cardiff lawyer, entered Parliament as Member for Pontypool, he was introduced to the House by the redoubtable Aneurin Bevan. They entered the Palace of Westminster through the great Hall where kings, queens and statesmen had walked when alive and lain in state when dead. Leo, a Welsh Jewish lad, was properly impressed and said so, perhaps a little too excitedly.

"Leo!" Nye Bevan is alleged to have scolded him. "If you are to get on here, you must cultivate irreverence."

I'd picked up the same message as our utility bus had passed "The Whore's Bed". Church College or not, the too reverent were going to be under pressure in Trinity. It was a message that was to be reinforced for me, night after night, over the next two years in the unofficial, impromptu and always scabrous concerts that took place in the "Smoke Hole", the only room in the building where people were allowed to smoke cigarettes.

The bus ground its way forward, turning right, out of Lammas Street, across the junction with Market Street and, in time, left, on to College Road. There was a gentle gradient. There were some fine houses, with carefully tended front gardens. There

Trinity and King Alfred's Colleges, Carmarthen, 1943-45. Back row. left to right: Stan, Olly. Seated: Cecil, Barry, Eric, Gordon, the outside-augmented 'Pembrokeshire gang'.

was one home whose garden hedges were geometrically and perfectly boxed. Whoever lived there had gone in for topiary, and a very large and leafy cockerel had been clipped out of a living tree. Inevitably, that male bird was a target for irreverence, too! "Cockadoodle do!" was the least of it.

Beyond the superior houses, there were high and unbroken hedges, and the inefficiently metalled road turned up hill. At once, we could see Trinity College, Carmarthen. We arrived at the pillared gateway and, turning left into the drive, ran alongside a flat-roofed three-storey, modern building that I was soon to learn to call "The Wing". After our day, it was grandly renamed, the Dewi Hostel. By 1996, it has been extended – a new block, another floor, a new, hipped-roof added – and been reconditioned to house a "state of the art" administration centre. The students now occupy modern apartment blocks.

In 1943, registration involved signing a form or so and, more significantly, a first meeting with a graciously formidable lady. The Principal's secretary was Miss Francis. She stood between us and the wrath or the approval of God on our very few journeys to the top of the side entrance-hall stairs in the twenty months or so of our residence. A frosted glass partition, set some distance back from the head of the stairs, had a sliding hatch at its centre. Miss Francis appeared at that hatch at the pressing of a bell-button. Few students crossed the threshold of the door to the left of the hatch. Beyond that door was the Principal's office. Miss Francis held the pass and kept guard over the Rev. Thomas Halliwell.

Rooms in the Wing were allocated to us. Our Pembrokeshire quartet came out of it rather well. Orsman, Owen, Parry and Parry came close alphabetically. I was next-door to my namesake and a near neighbour, on the second floor, to the other two. Among the "O's", too, was a then unknown David "Ollie" Oliver, from Aberystwyth. By such administrative chances, life-long links are made, although I've totally forgotten how Alan Stanford, from Wokingham, in Berkshire, came to be an honorary Pembrokeshire man and our inseparable companion.

Designed by that Jack-and-Master-of-all-Trades, architect and handicraft lecturer H. L. Harby, the Wing provided student accommodation that was very much up with the times, if not ahead of them, in what seemed, to me, then, reasonably spacious rooms. Mine – and all the others – had a wash-basin with hot and cold running water; a hot-water radiator; a three-ply wardrobe; a table, over which there hung an adjustable reading-lamp; a single, hospital type, iron-railed bed; and there was a yard and a half by a yard of mat on the red painted, polished floor. The windows were curtained with "black-out" material. Our living-space was as good as most of us enjoyed at home. The radiator, the wash-basin and hot and cold water were an improvement in style and in substance for me.

Our Neyland Manse had no bathroom. Washing water – carried in cans from the John Street "standard", usually by me, in my teen years – was boiled in the scullery "copper". The toilet – with no water laid on, and cut squares of old newspaper spiked on a nail behind the door – was at the bottom of the long garden. I had no complaints about my "digs" at Trinity.

Nor did it take long for any of us to unpack our cases or to hang our clothes. The wardrobe was more than large enough. We'd personalise our places as the months went by. For the moment, checking the lay-out of the College was the priority. Ronnie Lawrence guided us.

The College building was 98-years-old when we first toured it. By then, the original, generous, neo-classical structure had grown out across its grounds. There had been ten acres of those when the then Bishop of St. Davids had laid the foundation stone, in July, 1847, for a college "designed to take sixty students" and which was to have "a suitable Chapel for religious Worship, residences for the Officers and domestic offices". Work on it had been finished by September, 1848, and, on 24th October, the completion of that work "was commemorated by a public service in the Parish Church of Carmarthen and a public meeting at the Institution". By the 24th November, Sir Thomas Philipps, of Picton Castle, was able to report: "The Officers are now appointed, the building is partly furnished, and several students have already been received."

Those students had room to move about in their splendid new "Institution". There were only twenty-two of them during the first academic year. Total numbers grew to forty-nine in residence during 1849. They were to remain between forty and fifty for many years. Although recruitment seems not to have been affected, student travel to and from their College was made easier by the arrival of Brunel's South Wales Railway's services – trains from London to and from Carmarthen – in 1852.

Ahead of the times, though, by almost a century-and-a-half, the fine new college already had its "Mission Statement". It was approved by the Anglican Church and by the Society for the Promotion of Christian Knowledge. The "children of the poor in Wales" were to be "provided with ... religious self-denying, earnest Teachers" who were "Trained and prepared for the work of instruction".

Neither I nor any other of my group of Pembrokeshire friends was burdened by the knowledge of that, though, as we made our voyage of discovery. Not feeling particularly religious, nor noted for self-denial at home, we were, nonetheless eager – excited, even – as we found our way around that day. We were, ourselves, in a real sense "the children of the poor in Wales" still. There was a chance that each of us had been taught, at one stage or another, by some of the earlier students of the "South Wales and Monmouthshire Training College", which didn't change its name to Trinity College until 1931. I had already had three years schooling by then and was in Standard One of the "Big Boys" at Neyland Board School.

We discovered that what we'd taken to be the front entrance to the College was really the back of it. The main building faced south. Its true entrance hall – though students were not encouraged to use it – was in that south face. Attractive to those who, as I do, like the neo-classical, its front elevation windows looked out on lawns graced, spectacularly, by two giant Chile Pines – the "Monkey Puzzle" trees. One of these great trees still stands guardian, in 1996. Its partner fell in a tempest some years ago.

The College Chapel, remodelled in 1931, was annexed to the original building's eastern wall, while the Principal's residence – in some senses equally hallowed ground! – buttressed the west walls.

From the under-used main entrance, the long, tiled South Hall led to the Cloisters, the open-air quadrangle of grass, flanked on all sides by covered walkways, and to the steeply raked, stone internal stairway that connected the older College with the newer buildings. As these had been added, their foundations – cut out of rising contours – had called for some fairly radical planning to keep communications intact. The inordinately steep stairs were the product of it.

Off the South Hall, the Dining Hall opened to the left, and the ante-chapel and the Chapel to the right. There was a stairway there to upper-floor rooms and redundant dormitories, while doors to left and right opened on to lecture-rooms, further along the Hall. I recall being, that day and in the days to come, intrigued by splendid large prints of Hogarth cartoons that hung on the walls of South Hall.

We found a very attractive library where we would spend some time in the months ahead. Pride of place in this Church establishment was clearly given to the remodelled chapel, but there was an ultra-modern "Broadcast Hall". "Wireless" was king of the media then. The British Broadcasting Corporation set the standards in information, entertainment and education, and Trinity College had responded to it, in the thirties, by equipping an auditorium with B.B.C. radio facilities capable of broadcasting concerts, plays and whatever met the demand. Ultimately, it would become the Dean Parry Hall.

Nor were the Chapel and the Broadcast Hall the only up-to-date features of the complex. There was a Swedish-type gymnasium with an evolutionary, rolling, North wall that could be opened to the weather, at the high point of the campus once known to students as "The Alps".

Various specialist buildings, from Trinity's immediate pre-war expansion programme, still relatively new to the eye, made up a "street" of workshops, lecture rooms and, even, a new shower block and toilet complex, to serve gymnasts, athletes and gardeners. This conduit joined the public road to Johnstown at the west gate.

I say "gardeners" because the College, from its earliest days, had specialised in a "prudent mixture of manual labour with sedentary employment". There was even a complaint from the first of Her Majesty's Inspectors to assess the regime. "It is not prudent", Mr. H. Longueville Jones had warned, "to expose young men, who are of necessity much under cover, and in rooms, the temperature of which is considerably raised by the heat engendered by their collective presence, to the sudden vicissitudes of a humid atmosphere and damp ground. The change is more than their frames can resist ..."

Rural scientists, environmentalists, green lobbyists, of Trinity, Mr. H. Longueville Jones should be your Patron!

Among the facilities found within the main complex was a wicker-chaired and wicker-tabled reception area in the North Hall and, freestanding from that building but connected into it, was the rather splendid Examination Hall. There was, also, that students' "sanctum", that no-go-area for staff, the "Smoke Hole", that was to become our theatre-in-the-round. Above all this (in several senses!) were the administration offices, the Principal's office and that eagle's eyrie, Miss Francis's domain.

The grounds were well tended. The Principal's walled garden was particularly pleasant, though out of bounds. There were green fields still, with a horse in one of them, and the pasture dropped away steeply from the south-front lawns before levelling out to meet the road and the railway line, where they ran through Johnstown, both far enough away to preserve a monastic calm and a convent quiet within the acreage of grass and gardens.

Even so, in clear cold nights of late Autumn, if you listened for it, you could hear the rumble of military traffic as it gear-changed on to the hill towards the Picton Memorial and, on such nights, the rattle of the rail wagons or the prolonged hooting of the engine whistle emphasised the quiet by breaking it.

Our 1943 intake of students numbered more than seventy. Our seniors, in 1942, had topped sixty. When we, in our turn, became seniors, in 1944, a further sixty or so students joined us. At any given time during our sojourn at Trinity, there were no more than 125 students, all of whom were in residence. Naturally, we came to know them all.

Before taking our first meal together on that September evening, we had to draw our rations for the week ahead. We kept them in half-biscuit tins that we'd brought from home.

Once our supplies had been issued, we were allocated space on the shelves in a lean-to alcove off the conduit between kitchen and Dining Hall for our tins. From then on, we collected those tins before each meal and returned them afterwards. It says something for the corporate morality of those war years that I don't remember many complaints of pilfering from those unlocked safes.

Unpilfered, those tins contained a full week's rations, no more and no less than what was available to any other individual in Britain. We would have been handed two ounces of butter, two ounces of lard, four ounces of margarine, eight ounces of sugar, two ounces of tea, four ounces of bacon, and one egg "if available". Ultimately, bread was rationed, too, available only on unit coupons. Probably, the lard would be returned to the kitchen for cooking purposes. Even sweets were on ration, and clothes available only on "dockets" – clothing coupons in a supplement to our Ration Books.

As we sat down, eventually, for our first meal in college, the pseudo public school and "varsity" patterns were reinforced. A prefect topped each of the many long tables. Plates were passed up to that prefect, who dished out the food and passed it back. Our senior-year people sat around him. They were a privileged bunch. Few of them, known to one another, probably friends, they basked that evening in a sort of respect from the rest of us that they would never know again. Teenagers, most of us, we were happy enough with the pecking order. There were, though, other and sterner men amongst us who were, perhaps, already looking askance at these time-warped Tom Brown's Schoolboys.

Far from where we sat – where, if this had really been the theatre that, in some respects, it was, the proscenium arch would have been – was an actual stage. On that stage, in faithful mimicry of the halls and habits of Oxford and Cambridge, was "The High Table". At it sat the men and, just occasionally, a woman or two, who were set to shape our lives. Over time, they were pointed out to us by the cognoscenti who made another high table out of the top end of ours.

The British education system of the early 1940s was imitative of itself to the point of incest. Each institution aped – and longed to be – the one above it. Thomas Arnold inhabited the hearts and minds and shaped the stances of vice-chancellors, principals, and primary school heads from Land's End to John O'Groats. In 1943, on the eve of the introduction of the most important revision of national education since Forster's Act had put it within reach of all, at elementary level, in 1870, Trinity College, Carmarthen, was probably more firmly locked into its own history and borrowed plumes than it had been at any time.

With the 1944 Butler Education Act waiting in the legislative wings, the past held centre-stage still in Trinity. The war had not only taken the bulk of its students away, it had robbed it of younger staff, too. Inevitably, and in common with schools, colleges and universities throughout the land, it had turned in on itself as the breeding-stock of its intellectualism narrowed and aged. Practices petrified rather than evolved. In a sense, the high drama of Arnold's Rugby had become pantomime in this little theatre of education in West Wales.

Not that I knew it! I was agog! Delighting in it all, I couldn't hear enough from my betters at the top end of the table. Back again among the chenille cloths and velvet curtains, smelling the camphor, I listened to their gossip as avidly as my mother and I had absorbed every sibilant syllable of Mrs. Samuel Davies's special knowledge of the Royals.

Children now are better informed about everything than we were then. Six-year-olds in long trousers hack into adults' computers and learn, early, about adultery, this planet's major preoccupation. Adolescents "surf" on Internet. They bring the world – with its perfections and imperfections – into their terraced-house bedrooms, while their parents sleep in front of that most archaic of all electronic apparatus, the passive-receiver – "T.V." No-one knows yet how much their hyperactive, precocious, upstairs communicators understand of what they know. There is no adult supervision – no policeman, no parent, no teacher, no pastor, no priest – to intercept Internet. The chain is off that Bible. Alien feet may be walking all over the culture, new generations suborned, but is there anyone to say "Possible?" or "Never!" or "Well! Whoever would have believed it?" – introducing the cautionary doubt essential to the discovery of the whole truth.

After all, it was Matthew Arnold who lamented, at his father's death, that his passing left "none to cry 'Halt!'" as the world trekked back from progress.

But, as the 2nd September, 1943, darkened through dusk, I knew nothing of any of that. Nor did I care. I'd risen to my feet with all the others as a door behind the High Table had opened and the Principal, The Rev. Thomas Halliwell – mortar-boarded, gowned, Roman-collared and black stocked – had come through it, followed by his academically accoutred staff. They'd taken off their head-gear. The Principal had said grace in Latin. We said "Amen", in unison, and sat down again. I was hungry. Over those next years, I was to be hungry all the time. That was to say something about the voraciousness of a healthy lad, growing to be a man, his changing metabolism and high energy output, but it was also to say a great deal about the daily College diet prepared by Mrs. "Mother" Owen, the College cook. As she said, "There is a war on, ewe know, isn't it?"

In time, our parents would supplement our fare. Food parcels were a feature of the war and became a fact of life for us. There was one notable occasion when one arrived for me, lashed into the same pack as my clean laundry. The packaging posed a problem. My goods and chattels had been wrapped in water-proofed brown-paper. Water-proofed brown-paper was a war-time phenomenon, too.

Several layers of paper were inter-leaved with sheets of fibre that had been stiffened with some form of pitch. The parcel was impermeable. It was also inpenetrable. Of course, if the outer string were cut, it would have unwrapped as intended. You couldn't do that very well during an English lecture, where Barry Owen and I had taken it, after I'd collected it at mid-morning break. We were ravenous for my mother's Marmalade Cake.

A wartime recipe – probably conceived because the Ministry of Food had stock-piled more oranges than it could keep fresh – had been adopted and adapted by my mother. It was delicious; habit-forming. We were addicted to it. As Llew Llewellyn's lecture began, we started on the shell of the parcel. It resisted every move. Writing notes with my right hand, I attacked it with my left, where it lay, on the bench, between Barry and me, on my sinister side and his dexterous one. He was contorting himself, in his efforts to bring his free hand to bear on the problem, into a human-limb reef-knot: "Left over right and under: right over left and under."

At one point, he stabbed the paper with the leg of his geometry dividers, pinning it to the seat, and giving us purchase on the parcel. We were making progress, but the thing was resistant. As I dragged on the pegged-down paper, there was a loud, ripping noise, suggestive of all sorts of discomforts. Even Mr. Llewellyn paused, clearly trying to locate distress. We stared blandly ahead, as though we'd not heard a thing, as the whole of the group switched attention to us. An innocent student sitting beside us blushed. Some guilty indiscretion of the past revisited his face, involuntarily. Blame for something other than had happened fell on him.

We were not through yet. Fibre doesn't tear easily across the grain. Ripping eructations erupted, several times, before there was a hole in the cover large enough to let a couple of fingers through, then – like mice gnawing into a cheese through the rind – we were into food. By the time the lecture ended, we'd devoured practically the whole of that lovely Marmalade Cake, in lumps small enough to be dragged through a rip in the fibre of about two inches across; a literal cake-hole!

That cake, succulent, soggy, was a credit to Lord Woolton's Ministry of Food, to Keeler's Marmalade and to Mam, but our premature consumption of it caused a week of problems for me. Marmalade, even when bonded into a cake, is stickily pervasive. I still leave my showering until after I've eaten my toast and marmalade for breakfast. Have you noticed how marmalade gets everywhere? Well! My laundry was full of it. What's more, it was coloured, here and there, with flattened cake-crumbs and strips of candied orange-peel.

I wore Marmalade Cake for a week. My Sunday-go-to-Chapel shirt was variegated, altered, modified. Its detachable collar, normally Robins-starched and pristine, hung limp around my neck, like a striped sock. My underpants were the greatest trial. In one day of wearing, they stained my skin a striped and gentle ginger wherever they touched it. I wonder why people talk of "a crumb of comfort"?

"Suffer from the wind, do you?" I asked the chap who'd been blamed for the noises we'd made, when I met him in the Smoke Hole, later in the week, and he blushed again. "It wasn't me, whatever it was!" he protested. "Are you sure?" I teased.

Cruel of me, wasn't it? But I had to be revenged on someone for the discomfort of my crumbed and marmaladed laundry and for the dyeing-in-the-wool on my nether regions. Fortunately, the point of the compass had missed my garments.

In the dyed-in-the-wool tradition of the College, our first supper done, we were to report to a large, upstairs lecture-room for "P.S." It was not a post-scriptum to the meal.

"P.S." stood for "Private Study". None of us was trusted to study alone. Schoolboys in residence, again, we reported for one hour of supervised study. On that first night, we were watched over by Mr. Charles "Charlie" Wilford, the headmaster at the College's Model Practising School in the town who also served as music tutor at the college. A long-faced, thinnish man, he had a phenomenal memory for names. At subsequent College reunions of students – notably at its huge centenary gathering in 1948 – he showed off his memory in style.

Amusingly, he got my name wrong at first meeting. My parents had given him a number of options: Samuel, after Samuel Evans, my mother's father; David, both biblically and patronally, was, they thought, appropriate, too. The third name on my birth certificate, Gordon, was my first and real name. I'd never found out whether I'd been so named, after General Gordon – who, as a young lieutenant of engineers stationed at Llanion Barracks, Pembroke Dock, had supervised the building of the Palmerston "folly" fort at Scoveston, near Neyland – or simply because it sounded Scottish enough for a second son born on St. Andrew's Day. Charlie Wilford simply read out the first name he came to.

It was of a pattern that we were registered for private study attendance and, even more so, that we were instructed to respond with the Latin "Ad sum" or, through a nominee, "Ab est", as we were ticked off.

Cecil was the Parry who came first on the roll. He shouted his presence. Mr. Wilford, not a formal man, shortened Samuel to Sam. "Sam Parry", he called. I didn't know what to shout. I settled for "Gordon Parry, Sir!" "Who's Gordon Parry?" Charlie asked. "Down here it says that your first name is Sam." He repeated, "Sam Parry."

Much to the amusement of my old form-mates, I shouted back "Ad sum, Sir!" and, in that moment I had been rechristened, re-identified for the whole of my time at Trinity. Even my old friends gleefully called me "Sam" and, fifty years later, white-headed and wrinkled strangers arrive on our doorstep to enquire of my wife: "Is Sam Parry in, please?"

Funnily enough, my wife, Glenys, took up the Wilford nomination when we went out together while I was at Trinity. In revenge, I called her "Cath", the diminutive of her second name, Catherine. For ten years, until our daughter was born in 1955 and christened Catherine Anne, we kept up the pet names that "cheerful Charlie" Wilford had prompted in 1943.

We were being quickly initiated into Trinity's traditions, many of them obsolescent. Some of them – Latin tags in a bilingual country, with Welsh the native tongue and English the language of the student majority in a college where the classics weren't taught – were archaic to the point of quirkiness but, whatever we'd gathered so far was nothing to the initiation to come, a few evenings later, when registration was completed.

Unexpectedly, the General Prefect appeared at the door. "Excuse me, Mr. Wilford, Sir", he said. "The Principal's compliments, Sir. Could you join him in his study, Sir? I'm to take over supervision of 'P.S.'"

"Carry on with your work, gentlemen", Mr. Wilford com-

Glenys Incledon and Gordon Parry, Cadet Hall, Neyland, 1948.

manded. "Do exactly as you're told by Mr. Fry." Was he grinning as he left the desk, handing over his chair to Dickie Fry?

I imagine so. The interruption over, we settled back to the practice, or the pretence, of study. It had become very quiet. Then the lights went out. Through the darkness, the General Prefect said: "On your feet, gentlemen."

As he said so, there were loud noises off. It was as though the German paratroopers, expected every day earlier in the war, had finally made it. We'd certainly been invaded. Voices were screaming at us in Welsh and in English to "Hurry! Hurry! Hurry!": "Brys! Brys! Brys!" – or was it "Raus! Raus" Raus!" – out of the doorway, down the stairs and along the South Hall. Still dangerously in darkness, we were herded beyond the ammoniac smell of the urinals, up the stone steps to the North Hall and, through it, out into the dusk.

We could see our herders now. It was obvious that Charlie Wilford had been grinning. This was a Billy Bunter of "a jolly jape", and our initiation was at the core of it. "Worse things happen at sea, in wartime!" So we bowed our backs to knotted towels, registered our mock terror, and ran into the Broadcast Hall. It was got-up as an Assize Court. We were, all of us and each of us, to be put on trial. Richard Fry, wigged and gowned, presided.

When my turn came to be arraigned, I was accused – totally falsely! – of talking too much and of using "dirty words". Who might have betrayed me is locked in history. Since I'd only been in the place for three days – had listened, for once, more than I'd spoken, and had given up swearing when I knew that I'd been accepted for a Church College that I'd expected to be holy – I protested my innocence robustly. Much good had it done. I was sentenced to "Shut up and drink one dessertspoonful of quinine – to wash out your mouth and to dry up your tongue."

Naturally, I took my punishment like a man. Never having heard of, much less tasted, quinine, I wasn't in the least afraid of it. My executioner filled the spoon from a green bottle. He raised the spoon. I opened my mouth. He poured in the liquid. There was nothing to it – for a second or two – as I swallowed it down.

A moment later, I wondered whether I'd swallowed my tongue and the medicine spoon. My mouth snapped shut, involuntarily. All the muscles in my cheeks shortened by inches. Inside my head, things were moving about that I hadn't known were there. My three false teeth – replacements for three real ones lost in doing a Roy-Rogers-on-Trigger approach to the ferry-boat one morning, to entertain the Neyland gang: I'd been unsaddled and had bitten a steel waterpipe in a bloody encounter with that inanimate object – grew in my mouth as that orifice shrank. There was no spit anywhere in there. The Sahara was damper than the back of my tongue. My uvula, my tonsils, my adenoids were gone, blown away in some sirocco sandstorm of the ears, nose and throat.

"That", said the executioner, "will teach you to dry up!"

He never said a truer word. For the second time in my life, I was speechless. It was a guarded secret in our house that "Sam" Parry had been born tongue-tied and had only begun to speak when a doctor cut the lesion that bound the tip of his tongue to the floor of his mouth. What a genie he'd let out of the bottle! Now, I'd been bottled again: green-bottled by quinine.

Seventeen years on, robbed of a voice, mouthing profanities soundlessly, I staggered away, my initiation done, my vocabulary rich but unutterable, tongue-tied again. Among the incensed and the wounded who had gone through their own forms of metaphorical circumcision, I made my way, dry as a stick, to my iron-railed bed on the second floor of the Wing where the mattress was iron-hard, too. Somehow, nevertheless, I felt that I'd passed a fundamental test of my fitness for survival in Trinity. I wonder, though, whether a returned prisoner-of-war had much to prove?

For some Freudian reason, deep in his wounded psyche, Cecil Parry, fifty years later, remembered nothing of the Private Study that became a public rout and near riot, but he did recall being singled out for "black-bottoming". He'd been seized, stripped, thrown across his own bed and been 'Cherry-Blossomed" with a boot-brush by "a band of thugs". Possibly, they were carrying out a sentence passed on him by the Initiation Court. Their thuggery was burnished on his anatomy, while the Initiation Ceremony was imprinted on my memory.

CHAPTER FOUR

The Bells

"Keeping time, time, time,
In a sort of Runic rhyme,
To the tintinnabulation that so musically swells
From the bells, bells, bells, bells."

Was Edgar Allen Poe ever a student at Trinity? Days and nights there began and ended with the bells. Hours, half-hours, ten-minute interludes, clanged to the bell. There was a clamouring bell on each floor of the Wing. There was another one at each strategic corner of the buildings used by us. Within days of moving in, we were living by the bell. Pavlov could have saved his dogs some spit if he'd followed us around. I wonder whether he ever fed them quinine?

But the whole of western Europe was regimented in 1943. There was no reason for a possé of young males – fighting fit but on deferred entry to their country's services at a crucial point in a world war – to protest the protracted tintinnabulation that had them tumbling here, there and everywhere. Bugles were blowing "Reveille" for some and "Last Post" for others in too many places, too often.

As I woke to the bell on 3rd September, 1943, thousands and thousands of young men – many younger than I was – were storming the beaches of Italy's Straits of Messina.

Dawn, for them, had been Zero Hour, and many of them would never see another. The mighty 8th army had moved up from North Africa and, as we grumbled over our first college breakfast, Milton Bracker, an American radio journalist, was reporting, "by wireless", from Allied Headquarters, that the Allies had "breached fortress Europe" as British and Canadian Troops "stormed over the narrow Strait". With that sort of symmetry that is never accidental, the 3rd of September was the fourth

Wartime photograph of the Parry family. Brother, Bryn, was 'away at the war'.

anniversary of our declaration of war with Germany, following the Nazis' invasion of Poland.

On that Sunday morning – thirteen years and nine months old – I had been in Bethesda. My father had been in his pulpit. Jack Davies, a young deacon and family friend, was in his car parked at the pavement in Frederick Street. He was there for a purpose. The Prime Minister, Neville Chamberlain, was to broadcast to the nation at 11.15 a.m.

Unusually for those days, and a sign of his relative affluence, as a fish merchant on Milford Docks, Jack had a car with "a wireless". There came a moment when Mr. Davies walked quietly into chapel. My father moved to the head of the pulpit steps. His deacon went to the foot of them. There was a murmured conversation; then Dad walked back to the pulpit lectern. There was an open leather and brass-bound Bible on it, and the lectern was faced with a wine-coloured cloth on which one of the Chapel's members had worked a text in gold braid. It read, "God is Love", emphasising, that sunny morning, that man is not.

"My dear friends", said my father in his gravest voice, "for the second time in the lives of many of us, we are at war with Germany."

The congregation gasped. Even though the declaration of war had been expected, and they'd known that the British "ultimatum" to Hitler had been due to expire at 11.00 a.m., as our morning service was starting, the fact was still a shock. No-one knew what this war might turn out to be. Throughout the decade, Nazi troops had – with growing arrogance and triumph – "blitzkrieged" the resistance out of neighbouring nations. If our war with Germany followed the pattern, Luftwaffe dive-bombers could be in the air now, flying westward. Conscious of the concern, Dad announced an alteration in the time of the evening service and the cancellation of Sunday School.

The Prime Minister – that hapless umbrella-man whose scrap of paper out of Munich had promised us "Peace in our time" – was set to eat his words in a second broadcast to the nation at 6 o'clock. My father, even though he'd set the evening service back, assumed that the majority of his members would be absent from it. He was wrong. His chapel was to be crowded to the door, that evening and for many wartime Sundays to come.

Without knowing it, my father had used, almost exactly, in his announcement, a sentence from Chamberlain's radio address –

without the quavering uncertainties of that sincere but discredited man – "for the second time in the lives of many of us, we are at war" he, too, had said.

"Therefore", said John Donne, "send not to ask for whom the bell tolls, it tolls for thee." Chamberlain fell, pushed from office. Churchill rose, propelled into it. The "phoney war" followed. Then came the Battle of Britain, and real war elsewhere. Two of the younger men, Clemmie Mathias and Leonard John, in chapel when my father announced the declaration of war, never came back from it. Jack Davies, though older, was commissioned and mentioned in dispatches for distinguished service. Bombs even fell on Neyland, killing all the women of one family in Hazelbeach. France and the Low Countries fell, and our harbour was filled with small craft – inshore fishing-boats, pleasure-craft, river-ferries – that had run before the storm of weather and the war to find shelter from both in Shakespeare's "fairest port of all".

Neyland's population swelled with refugees, evacuees and soldiers, sailors and airmen. High Street, Neyland, echoed to a babble of foreign languages. Dutch, Belgian, Polish, Canadian and American English, French – even Italian, in time, from prisoners-of-war, who were set to working on the farms – added their influences to the bilingualism of West Wales.

I'm not the only one alive today who recalls the moment when Mrs. Wheeler, whose one-and-only language was Honeyborough-local, brought her fifteen-stone body, in its tightly-trussed, new, green Women's Voluntary Service uniform to an undulating halt in front of Billy Nash the Butcher's window. She had in tow three ladies who were as large as she was. Newly arrived, on their husband's coastal fishing-boats, out of their overrun Belgian seacoast villages, they were being helped to settle into our little town. Mrs. Wheeler clearly had no problems in communication. Indicating the lean, wartime-under-rations provenance in Mr. Nash's store, she said, in her fog-horn voice: "an' zis is zee zhop ver you buy zee meat."

Three scarved heads bobbed up and down in time with hers and three loosely-corsetted bodies rippled with more poundage than Billy Nash had quartered in a fortnight.

There was, too, a house-party that was treated to a tearful, elongated rendering of "Hi-ron-dell-ell-er-er-er!" by the young French wife who had seen the swallow on the bottle of cheap and cheerful Barsac that was being passed around. Her hostess, a fan of Roy Rogers and Qui-me Sabe, had no problem with foreigners, either. Tapping the Barsac, she said: "Bottle speak". He say: "One for the road, is it?" The Plaza Cinema had its part to play in making allies comfortable in Neyland!

By the time of our residence at Trinity, one of the largest concentrations of United States troops in the country had begun to build up in the hutted fields around Glangwili, on the outskirts of Carmarthen: the troops preparing for their own landings on the beaches of Europe, and specialist medical units moving in to a prefabricated, state-of-the-art, field hospital – literally in the fields – making ready to receive their broken bodies, if or when they were to be struck down, as so many were to be, on the unwelcoming beaches of the continent.

"Fortress Europe" having been "breached", a long, left-wing campaign to "open the 2nd Front now", to take the weight off the besieged Vatican city of Communism, Moscow, and brave, beleaguered Stalingrad, wouldn't be frustrated much longer.

Joe Davies, our coalman, who actually carried the coal that Samuel Davies had factored, humped a one hundredweight sack of it up our long garden path every week. He had a cleft palate – in days when plastic surgery was not nearly as clever as it is now. His day's nasal announcement dismayed my mother. "'Possible! Mr. Davies", she exclaimed. "Not two shillin' a bag, surely?" "Sorry, Ma'am", he said, down his nose. "It's the war. There's a war on. Everything's goin' up, an' the miners 'ave to live, too." Joe looked like a miner; patinad with coal dust, diamonded with carbon, sweating, glinting, in the morning sun.

His was a clever defence. Dad had been a miner. Mam's brothers were mine-workers who had not only cut coal but had shaped the National Union of Mineworkers to fight for better treatment for them. Mam elected to settle blame on the war. "Sooner this blessed old business is over", she said, taking a solid, silver florin from her real leather purse, "the better it will be for all of us."

Dad, who was standing on the back doorstep, said: "We seem to be winning now, at last, Mr. Davies." The Nazis were on the run in North Africa.

"Yes, Boss", he said. "The Germans say that they're 'retreatin' accordin' to plan' but it's our bloody plan now, i'nit? If you'll forgive the language, Ma'am?"

A preacher who'd cut coal and a minister's wife who had

washed the backs of colliers, home from their stint at the coal-face, weren't going to be shocked by a "bloody" or two from their coal-man but they noted it, editing the comment into the never-to-be-printed book of family anecdotes for winter evenings.

"Funny thing is", my father told his younger son, who used the word in every out-of-adult-hearing, back-lane sentence – even injecting it between syllables in some words, like "abso-bloody-lutely" – "is that his 'bloody' has nothing to do with blood. It is the corruption of an ancient Christian, Catholic oath. Crusaders used to swear 'By Our Lady!' It became 'B' Our Luddy'. 'B' Luddy', and now it's bloody." Secretly, the lad was bloody glad to hear that. It made his own use of the word less of a betrayal.

Indeed, the night before the Messina landings, settling into my cast-iron bed, I had heard the first of the College curfew calls. At 9.50 p.m., the bell had shattered the silence. As its ringing died away, I heard a stentor of a prefect making his way along the corridor, shouting, "One man, one room! One man, one room!" and repeating it in Welsh, "Un dyn, un ystafell! Un dyn, un ystafell!" The din of his authority had hardly died away when exactly at 10.00 p.m., the bell rattled the place again, and the guardian of our sleeping arrangements was back.

This time, he was representing not only Trinity and its determination to keep its students apart overnight but he was ensuring that they should be alone in the dark. "Allan a'r golau!" "Allan a'r golau!" "Lights out!" "Lights out!" Apparently, they weren't going out fast enough along the way. "Allan a'r bloodi golau", he shouted – his personal crusade and his crusader's oath taking on some asperity. "Put that bloody light out!" "We're retreating according to somebody else's plan now!" I said to myself, down my nose, in the dark. Then, perhaps, because I could hear my mother's voice saying, "Shame on ewe! Ewe'll be stuck like that one day, my boy! Mockin' the afflicted!" I said my prayers. Then I turned on to my side and was lost.

The day had been so tumultuous, its hours filled with so much, that I seemed scarcely to have dropped off when the bell shook the building again. It was morning already. The powers that were wanted us all up and about. Allowing for time-zones and adjusting "Zero Hour", I could have been stripped naked, sluicing at the sink, as the men and boys of Messina, soaking from the sea, took the land war into Italy, "the soft, underbelly of the Axis". At the time, I knew nothing of that. When the news broke, it didn't really affect our immediate lives very much. Within half-an-hour of that first bell, we were due at the dining-hall, half-biscuit tins at the ready; little battles of our own to fight.

That night, in the Smoke Hall, I would be introduced to the College's corrupted version of "There is a happy land, far, far away". There was a long, strong and probably very valuable oak-table in the terracotta-tiled, low-ceilinged room. That once white, now yellow, ceiling, condensed and concentrated nicotine for us as the smokers smoked for dear life and non-smokers, such as I was, filled their lungs with what wouldn't, for years, be recognised as a passive passport to a shorter life. Non-smokers were the social oddities then. Woodbines, Players, Camels, even, and the rather camp, cork-tipped and expensive Egyptian Sobranis, were clouding the air about us all. The oak-table was the theatre stage, and the Master of Ceremonies was already up on it. The utterly unofficial, augmented College choir was about to break into a ritual four-part harmony.

> "There is a training coll.' far, far away,
> Where they eat bread an' jam three times a day.
> Oh! Hear them laugh and sing
> As the bread an' jam comes in
> Oh! How they laugh and sing, three times a day."

By some sort of random choice, I would find myself standing among tenors musical enough to carry me into high harmony. I'd always fancied myself a bath-time Caruso but had difficulty in holding a tune. Mind you, I always bathed in a tin bath in front of the fire at home – scalding hot on one side, draughty on the other – after my sisters had gone to bed and before my brother took it over. So the uncertainties, the variations of pitch, could perhaps be excused. My immediate neighbour in the sing-song – a good musician – would be John Evans. Not the tallest man in that crowded choir, he was from Aberdare. We'd met earlier in the day, in passing – give or take a vowel! – at the crowded, communal watering-hole known as "The Bogs".

There were no toilets in the Wing. There were, as I've said, wash-basins in the rooms. H. L. Harby once grumbled to his

"Advanced" woodwork and metal-work group, to which I belonged, that he couldn't understand why all the copper connections of the down-pipes on the flat face of the Wing had turned green. "They're pea-green", he said. "Though I'm not certain which pee-green they are." He was certain, of course. Tradition is tradition.

As a footnote to hygiene and clean habits, there were no washbasins in the toilets in 1943. I don't know how many scaled several flights of stairs, retracing their journey, to wash their hands as the bell summoned them, urgently, to breakfast. I know I didn't. It seems incredible now. I've been fastidious for fifty years but, in our John Street Manse, the only in-house water-tap ran with rain-water that had been collected in the troughs along the roof and stored in a cement-lined static "tank" abutting the scullery. In warm days and summer weather, the tap above the scullery sink – my father called the sink "the bosh" – not only delivered water that was warm but little white and lively threadworms as well. Anyone tempted into nostalgia for some sort of rural Welsh Arcadia should know that it never existed. Life in the countryside – free and easy, uncomplicated though it was – was never sanitary. There were as many bluebottles as roses round the door. Country gardens smelled of other things than night-scented stock. There seemed little point in washing your hands in warm-worm-water. Nor did any of us then use deodorant or after-shave lotion.

My father – a dedicated visitor of the sick – used an oderant, not a deodorant. He washed himself down twice daily in diluted Lysol and sweetened his breath with broken peppermints. "Well! We're told to watch – and pray", he'd say, with a grin. "No point in catching something when you can wash it away with Lysol."

What with his Bay-rummed hair, his pocketful of peppermints, and the heady scent of disinfectant from his Lysol bottle, he could well have killed all the bacteria within fifteen feet of him. His members who were ill welcomed his visiting. His prayers and his presence, they said, did them good: a praying, air-freshener in himself, he remained free of infection, no matter where he'd visited, and no-one's sickness frightened him away. If there'd been a leper colony in Neyland – as once there had been – he'd have braved it with his Lysol bottle and his faith.

At Trinity, breakfast, on 3rd September, was eaten off the same table-cloths that had covered the tables at our first supper on the 2nd. No longer clean, they would remain where they were for the whole of the week. Cursory hand-brushing notwithstanding, they would gather to themselves a rainbow of discolouration from breakfast, dinner, tea and supper droppings for the next six days. By 9th September, there would be as much protein in the table-cloth as there was in the meal. It was already rumoured that Mother Owen made Tuesday's broth from Monday's laundry-washing water, and it was known – bruited down from the nearer tables to them – that the Staff's food was set on fresh, blanched linen for almost every meal.

There was, in that disparity, in that dining-room, on those grubby table-cloths, in the kitchens that served them and in the wide age-range of the students eating there – as early as our first week – the beginnings of a problem for the administration. They wouldn't recognise the problem for a long time. Nor would they admit that there was one when they did. "Those times they were a-changing", and, as the man said, "all change hurts someone, even when it's from good to better."

There was an aggravant to the problem. Every student, we'd learned, had to report, in his turn and as often as twice a month, for "kitchen duty". They were blackmailed into it. "There is a war on, you know. If you were in the services…!" So we left our beds long before the wake-up bell rang and reported to Mother Owen on our nominated day for what the service-men called "Jankers".

For the whole of the day, lectures were set to one side as we washed the dishes, peeled the potatoes, uncaterpillared the cabbages and, generally, did the chores. It wasn't what Samuel Davies would have had in mind for this son of the manse. "D'you think it's right, a minister's son skivvying?" he might have said, but there was no resigning from there.

Indeed, it was not unpleasant, a break from the lecture-room, and the positives were there, too. We had as much as we wanted to eat – an eye-opener in itself – and we learned for ourselves just how abysmal the back-stage catering was. Kitchen staff were few but, for those who were paid to work there, there was a hidden bonus. They lived pretty high on the hog. They didn't tote their rations about in half-biscuit tins. Rationing scarcely existed for them. The more often we did duty with them, the stronger the suspicion grew that The High Table didn't do badly, either. We had become a fifth column, accidentally, into espionage, gathering information for the struggles of the future: not evidence perhaps, of a black market but the sound of a grey "fiddle" or two in the corporate band.

When we were following the bells, on our first morning at lectures, we were summoned by them to two one-hour sessions; sent by them for a ten-minute, mid-morning break, which became much more important as the days went by because "Mail Call" took place then, and we were given any letters that might have arrived for us. We attended another two one-hour seminars after the break and presented ourselves again, famished, at the dining-hall for lunch.

Our curriculum covered three main groupings of subjects. These were classified as Professional Courses, Courses of Ordinary Standard, and Courses of Advanced Standard. Generally, we chose among them on a basis of our results in our Central Welsh Board School Certificates at "Ordinary" or "Higher". I'd been following higher-level courses in English, Geography and Woodwork at school. I opted for Geography and Handwork at advanced level in College. There was, also, Religious Education, the teaching of which was shared by Captain Ithel Thomas and, the College Chaplain, the Rev. Mr. Fountain.

Then, there were the "professional" subjects. These were compulsory for all of us, and all of them were taught to the entire College year – the total roll – in lecture sessions. With a diminished staff – seven only who were full-time, and two, Charlie Wilford and Mrs. Dr. Humphreys, who were part-time – there were no tutorials. Except in practical subjects, we never broke into groups. We attended lectures and took notes, 75 of us at a time.

When our year – class of '43-'45 – settled down to study, I was committed to attending lectures on the principles and practice of education, health education, physical training, and English language, as "professional" courses; to English literature, as a course of "ordinary standard"; and to geography and hand-work at "advanced" standard.

Impressive though the list might seem in retrospect, I didn't, during that first week, nor at any time, save, perhaps, in the week or so before final examinations, feel burdened down by it. Studying – although I'd been brought up with a father who used our middle room as a study and spent every Wednesday at our draw-leaf dining-table, because our middle-room was also our dining-room when we had visitors, studiously preparing his Sunday sermons – had never been a pre-occupation of mine. Reading had.

Since Miss Le Huquet, the lovely blonde, blue-eyed daughter of immigrant Channel Island parents who, happily lives still, as Mrs. Ivy Morgan – had held my index finger to the line of print as we chanted together individual letter sounds and whole words in the "Look and Say" method of teaching children to read, revealing the mystery and releasing the magic of the fun, phonetics and vowel sounds that made words speak on paper, I'd been a reader.

"Possible if ewe've finished that book already an it's not dinner time, yet?" my mother would say on Christmas morning. Although she meant "Impossible", it was wholly possible. Books were as compulsive an addiction for me as videos are for children today. When my parents came to bed, not shouting "Allan a'r bloodi golau" but taking the candle on its candlestick away from my bedroom mantelpiece, I used to wait awhile. Then, I'd get out of bed, wrap myself in the counterpane and sit with my back to the window, inside the curtains, reading there by our street gas-lamp, often until Bertie Snow, the lamplighter, set his short ladder against the lamp-post's crossbar and shinned up it to pull the chain that turned it off.

Come to think of it, at least for those clandestine hours after lights-out in our house, the chain was off my Bible, too! I read "No Orchids for Miss Blandish" there – on counter-balancing, counter-paned nights – after a girl-friend had found it under someone's bed and loaned it to me. Talk about "behind the bike shed!"

And I had a good memory. Early, my father, a reciter himself, had had me commit poems to memory. He'd volunteer me to recite them at Sunday School Anniversary – that Palace of Varieties of the Chapels of Wales – at Band of Hope, at Young People's Guild and at the annual eisteddfodau, where the Neyland schools – Sunday, Board, and Church Voluntary schools – showed off their talents and competing scholars. Wales was a forcing-house then for all the talents. Anglicised though south Pembrokeshire was, its native-born were Welsh-in-English, adopting traditions of a culture older than that the strangers had brought in.

So, at Trinity, the time-table, the studying, didn't seem obsessive. In my group, no-one semed oppressed by it. We delighted, though, in the afternoon activities. As I remember, we were free after lunch, to specialise. Specialisation included the practical work in our chosen subjects. Some of us spent more time than was demanded in the superbly fitted wood and metal workshops. Making cigarette lighters out of Army badges and copper pipes was popular. Others developed their talents in drawing and painting, preparing portfolios. Often, even the clanging of the bell failed to rip us away.

I also had a secret occupation all to myself. There was a locked connecting door in the wall of the metal-work room. Borrowing his bunch of keys from the temporarily unattended work-bench of the craft assistant, I discovered a "Marie Celeste" of a room behind it. There must have been forty desks in there, and each one housed a Remington typewriter. I cut myself a key and, over the months, taught myself to two-finger type.

Then, there was the sport. Eric Orsman, Barry Owen, Cecil Parry were bouncers of the round ball in the various forms. In time, two of them were to represent the College, either in hockey or soccer. In theory, I was a rugby man, but not yet in practice. My brother, Bryn, had played for Neyland "All Blacks" at seventeen years of age before joining the Ordnance Survey at Southampton. He was, in the 1940s, captain of the Rugby XV at Catterick Officers' Training Unit and played for the Royal Corps of Signals and the Combined Services XV. By the time that I'd been old enough to emuluate him, Neyland Rugby Club, with all its players "called-up", had all but adjourned "for the duration". Our secondary school, during my time there, played soccer only, during the winter term. There were more than eleven players better than I. The closest that I'd got was keeping goal for Picton House. At Trinity, I became a "Harrier".

The Harriers were the College's long-distance runners. Once a week, on Wednesday afternoons, they ran practice races against one another. I joined them, discovering that I could keep up with all but the best of them on the eight-mile canter out of the campus, down-hill to Johnstown, along what was then the A40 main road to Pembrokeshire, to where – years in the future – the Three Counties Showground would be built – and, then, turning right down a brambled lane and out on to the moors towards Trevaughan. Almost an hour later, mudded from head to foot on most mid-week afternoons, we'd gallop back on to

College Road, exhilarated. The steaming shower and the languid gossip followed. I was delighted to be chosen to represent Trinity in the first and in every subsequent fixture of my years there! We competed as a team – at home or away – on a Saturday.

Carmarthen town took pride, as well it might, in two splendid cinemas. They were the "Capitol" and the "Lyric". We patronised, if we were in funds, both of them each week. We were allowed to do so on a Wednesday afternoon and could please ourselves on a Saturday evening – subject to being in the College Chapel in time for Compline!

With one thing and the other, our daily and weekly schedule kept us busy. The ringing of the bells kept us on course.

By the time we gathered for the "Smoke Hole" concert on our second evening in College, we had some concept of how crowded our days were going to be. We were, I think, supercharged with anticipation: slightly different from one of the classes that Barry Owen dismissed in my presence when we taught, years later, in adjoining rooms at the brand-new "New School" – so new that it hadn't been named the Sir Thomas Picton School – at Haverfordwest. Barry had been enthusing on space travel – a passionate interest of his – to the fourteen-year-olds when the bell had rung for them to move on. "There they go", he said, "agog with indifference". That second night in the "Smoke Hole" – wreathed in other people's smoke – we were anything but indifferent.

Enquiries had been made for new talent, and there was to be plenty of it discovered among my contemporaries. D. H. G. "Gwyn" Davies, of Merthyr Tydfil, was there. Wonder of wonders, he was a film actor already! He had played the son – the boy-fighter and juvenile lead – in "How Green Was My Valley!" We touched the hem of his garment and expected great things from him. For the early concerts, though, it was our seniors who did their party-pieces, and very, very good they were.

This group was male, chauvinist, quick-witted, free from supervision other than by its peers, and far away – most for the first time – from the sanctions of Mam and Dad and "What will the neighbours say?" Talk about cultivating irreverence! The Smoke Hole rang rich with it. Satire was already gathering an audience in Trinity when David Paradine Frost was only four-years-old.

Some of the sketches had been handed down over the years.

Some of the songs – stolen from Sankey with words amended from Moody, by some Robert W. Service of the valleys – topical war-songs with dirty words, were popular. And, of course, standards of singing, real musicianship in unaccompanied solos, duets, quartets and augmented choruses, were often at least semi-professional. Best of all were the impromptu remarks from the packed audience. I ached with laughter at some of them, laughing myself to tears with the unexpected raffishness of it all, before I found my own throat to heckle. Church College! I'd been misinformed about Anglicans!

There were serious, patriotic moments, too, usually breaking through in a rendering of "We'll Gather Lilacs in the Spring Again" or "There'll be Blue Birds over the White Cliffs of Dover". We were not wholly thoughtless of the world-at-war outside. Nor did we ever forget to sing the time-honoured Trinity anthem, "There is a tavern in the town, in the town".

Then, as the bell clashed, again, for the twentieth time that day, to signal that another day was over, we'd be into the dithyramb, our passionate, choral hymn in honour of our College of the triune God and of Mother Owen, with its ultimate chorus: "Oh! How they laugh and shout as the bread and jam comes out, three times a day!"

Finally, there was the crush in the doorways and on the stairs, pushing and shoving to be one man in one room before "Lights Out". Quiet came down, at last, on the long corridors of the Wing, but all hell was let loose on the roads to Messina.

CHAPTER FIVE

The Staff

In those early days in Trinity, meal-times were briefing-times. They were almost the only ones when we sat down with our seniors. They enjoyed showing off their knowledge to us. We enjoyed harvesting it from them.

An early surprise had been that there were two colleges rather than one under the Trinity roofs. The regally-named King Alfred's College, Winchester, evacuated from Hampshire, was being hosted at that stage of the war in Carmarthen. In fact, by 1943, the Colleges had all but amalgamated. We ate together, worked together, played in representative teams together and, if it hadn't been for the presence of the Rev. R. C. White – Principal of King Alfred's – at the High Table, around the College as a "presence" and as a lecturer in history, it would have been difficult to know.

There was a third college using the campus, too. Wycliffe College was, actually, a public school: that is, a public school of the private kind. Evacuated, too, using, perhaps only occasionally surplus college accommodation, we only saw pupils in transit or on the rugby field when they played other schools.

In the earliest months of the war, there had been a wholesale evacuation of schools and colleges out of England into Wales. Rural Carmarthenshire had seemed – and proved to be – a safe haven. It would be interesting to know, if detailed records exist, how many school-age evacuees were educated in Carmarthenshire between 1939 and 1945.

In Trinity, I was conscious of only three or four Alfredians in our year. Several of them were reasonably remarkable and all of these had been evacuated twice, having fled before the German occupation of the Channel Islands.

Truly remarkable among these was the "mature" student Peter Cherry, who came to the College in 1943 as a rather mysterious addition to our ranks and, in a way, never left it. Brilliant, educated already far beyond our general level, he was recruited to the staff of Trinity after two years as a student, serving as a lecturer for a number of years before being found dead, of natural causes but quite unnaturally young, in his college apartment.

In his days as our student contemporary, this quiet but very charismatic man – lean, almost Germanic in his features and his sandy-blonde colouring, erudite, trilingual and pleasant – attracted a group of people around him who seemed almost to be his disciples. They were bright people, too, always moving about the place together. I never found out why this very able man should have turned up when he did in what had become a backwater academe offering qualifications to teach that were, presumably, below the level of his own academic potential.

Inevitably, since there was no real information to digest, we made menus of our own. Sensing a novel, some of us, quite scandalously, had him for a "sleeper", an undercover agent for the occupation forces of the 3rd Reich, whose Panzers might, even yet, sweep into Wales. Others saw him as a former German staff officer who'd read the runes and gone to ground early. Speculation about the man was probably as unjustified as the often toted story that Dean Parry, The Very Rev. Mr. Dean of St. Davids Cathedral, a former Principal and present grey eminence of the place, had been seen giving Mother Owen a large bottle of bromide to add to our tea, to temper our lustiness. People, such as former Army Sergeant John Rees, claimed that they could taste it. "We had it in our tea, all the time", they'd say. "How else could you keep the lads' minds on the war when they were marching through France?" Some of us did spend undue time in Woolworths ogling "the talent" behind the counters there. I can't say that I noticed either the taste or the triumph of bromide.

Dean Parry was alleged to be the puppet-master of Trinity then. The strings of control at our College, it was said, ran all the way back to his deanery in St. Davids. Christopher Wren and Anthony Trollope, together, might have designed this man. The head by Wren, the rest of him – physique, wardrobe, and religious-political involvement – by Trollope; he was a walking anachronism.

I've no idea how old the Dean was, but he looked as old as God. His black-beetle outfit, everywhere buttoned tight on to his spare frame, topped his little legs, in their velvet gaiters, punched by patent fasteners from his knee-caps to his patent leather shoes. A Roman collar, built for a bigger neck than his, only slightly relieved the funeral black of his clothes. His slender neck rose, retracted, rotated, in that collar, as his eyes went here, there and everywhere. Sunken themselves in a ruff of eyebrows and eyelashes, they missed nothing. Above those brows rose the rest of his head – and there was much of it – a bony operculum rounding up into the dome of St. Paul's that housed the brain of the Dean of St. Davids. Trinity trembled at his coming, I believe, and lesser men acknowledged the quality of that brain.

I know nothing of him other than his reputation. A King Alfred's student, actually named King, negotiating the black-out seal of the boxed, back entrance to the North Hall, with his drawing-board heaped with his art-class material – his inks, brushes and paints – swung his arms upwards and over and out, at precisely the moment that the very reverend gentleman had been coming in! The board's corner, catching him somewhere between his collar and his crotch, sent the Dean sprawling. He lay on his back, his little legs and shining shoes kicking in the air, a black beetle on its carapace, upside down. Rhonchus rattlings and whistlings snored from him. If anything needed the kiss of life, it was that winded old princeling of the Church. No-one knew how to give the kiss of life then, but there might not have been volunteer kissers if they had. He was fussed over, of course, but his breath had to come back on its own. He was last seen being half-carried up the stairs to Principal Halliwell's office. Crisis clouded Carmarthen.

The student, King, acting the tragic, student prince, made a dramatic round of farewells to his friends in the joking but half-serious "certainty" that his own career among us was over. "I'll suffer the wrath of God for knocking down His Dean", he claimed. "If he dies, it'll be manslaughter! I'll do time! They'll surely rusticate me, anyway, won't they?"

None of that happened. Nothing was ever heard again of the incident, painful though it must have been to the cleric's health and dignity. He was, perhaps, nothing like the reputation that had attached itself to him. It was reported, though, by our fifth-columnists of the kitchen that he seemed to have taken away from the College more than he'd brought in. Perhaps it was ipecacuanha wine to loosen his chest or wintergreen to rub into his bruises: or was it a plump, roast chicken?

Principal Halliwell was nothing like his mentor. A rubicund north-country man and sometime Parish Priest, he was in a second period of residence at Trinity College. Apparently, he'd been recruited originally as a lecturer, become a clerk in holy orders, "gone north", as men of talent in Wales do! and then returned as College Chaplain. Clearly influenced by his Principal, he had emerged as his successor when the Dean won preferment in the Church. He hadn't, by 1943, escaped from the shadow of his predecessor.

The mantle of College Chaplain, once about the shoulders of Principal Halliwell and former Principal Parry, was worn, during 1943 and early '44, by the Rev. Mr. Fountain, a quiet, pleasant priest – a teacher and a preacher – who left for other service when the academic year ended. His place was filled by the Rev. Stanley Moss, M.C.

Major Moss came home to us from the war, a warrior-padre, awarded high battle honours and carrying the scars of his service in a lame leg – complicated by "the King's Evil", scrofula – that, bandaged tightly from knee to ankle, slowed him in his ascent of the pulpit steps, but in little else. As his Principal was, a North of England man, he was younger, leaner, quicker, direct and blunt. The students of the tucked-away Trinity – time-warped, woofed and sheltered from the battling world on their "deferred service" – sat up and took notice as, leaning on the pulpit rail, his military badges and martial insignia as prominent on his vestments as the cross that adorned them, the veteran vicar of Christ introduced himself.

"You'll find me a plain man. I call a spade a spade an' there 'ave been times, these last years, when I've called it 'a bloody shovel'."

George Bernard Shaw and "Pygmalion" had put our coal-man's back-yard oath – and my back-lane one – into the mouth of Eliza Dolittle and passed it on to a wider circulation, but Stanley Moss still caused some College consternation when he brought the warring Crusaders' "By Our Lady" swearing back to its origins in the Christian Church.

There was one other member of staff who joined the faculty at Trinity in the Autumn Term of 1994. He was the already well-known and destined to be better known, Jac L. Williams. Sadly, since we were "down-below", South Pembrokeshire lads and "Cymru di-Gymraeg", we were not taught by him. Politically a nationalist, he was to have an enormous influence in the years ahead, in alerting a new generation to the threatening demise of the Welsh language and to the central rôle of that language in the total culture of our nation. Moving to Aberystwyth's University College of Wales and to a bigger stage, he helped to focus the minds of the non-Welsh speakers, as well as those born into the mother-tongue, on Welsh language and literature. Never physically robust – not in 1944 or later – dark in colouring, pallid in complexion, he was probably as formative a figure as any in turning Trinity – with its high Anglican traditions and teaching – firmly towards its later vocation as a crusading college, strengthening its dedication to the Welsh heritage, to the language, to the literature and to giving confidence in their Welshness to the teachers going out from there into a largely apathetic range of class-rooms and staff-rooms in South Wales and elsewhere. The fight for "yr hen iaith" was to take on a sharper edge, honed by the commitment of the quiet academic who shared a year with us through 1944 into 1945.

The Principal, however, was not noticeably political. A kindly man, comfortable, physically rounded, intellectually alert and still studying, he lectured us in Divinity and tried out on us some of the stuff that he was writing on the significance of dreams. A vicar, I think, at heart, he seemed – attractively – still rather surprised to have been the dauphin, much less the king. A goldfish, moved into a bigger bowl, grows bigger no matter how old. Principal, the Rev. Thomas Halliwell, still young, was growing into his new bowl, even if former Principal Parry still stirred the water from time to time.

A college for males only, monastic still, with all men between 18 and 36-years-old subject to national war-service "call-up", Trinity couldn't have been an exciting place in which to teach. There were only two members of staff who looked remotely as if they were under 40. These were the English lecturer, Mr. "Llew" Llewellyn, and the much more rumbustious physical education lecturer, Mr. David Griffiths – Britain's Olympics team gymnast – invariably known as "Dai Griff".

Mr. Llewellyn seemed unlikely to be fit for military service. Bespectacled, chesty and suffering chronic catarrh, gentle and gentlemanly, with all the Welshman's love of and admiration for the English language, which he spoke heavily accented with his own, he seemed infinitely more fitted to lecture to potential warriors than to go to war himself.

Dai Griff, on the other hand, who had been to one Olympics and, but for the war, would have been picked for another, was, in all but one aspect, as fit as a flea. Gerald, the Welshman, had described his countrymen as short, strong in the shoulders, bred to fight. David Griffiths was all of that. He was dark, too, raven-haired and aquiline. He was probably a throw-back to the Silures who'd fought the Romans for the better bits of Wales.

Only one thing could have kept Dai Griff out of the fighting forces, we assumed. Suited in almost every way to be a Marine Commando or a Special Services parachutist, he had only one deficiency. He couldn't see across a small room. Without his pebble-thick glasses, he could scarcely see at all. The army's loss was our gain. The modern gym became something of a fitness club for us. Our sports preferences – all that running for me – were toughening us up. The complicated gymnastics loosened us up.

As members of Dai Griff's advanced P.T. group, being prepared by him for a prestigious education display in the Brangwyn Hall, Swansea, we were given a shattering demonstration of the curse that his myopia was to this superb athlete. We understood, after that, why he had – while being a member of the team – not actually competed in the Games.

He was teaching us the "Flying Angel" vault. Perhaps his choice of that particular one was cocking a gentle snook at the Anglican establishment of Trinity. It involved two pieces of apparatus. One was the "Buck", the wooden horse. The other was an elastically-sprung launching canvas. The vault involved us in a dynamic take-off from this "trampoline", a giant leap high over the box, and an unfurling of our "angel's wings", our arms and legs, starred and at full extension, before a sharp "cut off", with bent elbows and knees, had us landing into a forward roll on the long mattress.

Potentially spectacular, it all took perfect timing. None of us was up to it. Dai Griff intervened.

As had many of his generation – Wynford Vaughan Thomas, Dylan Thomas, "Geevers" Jones – David Griffiths had worked hard to acquire a "standard English" accent. B.B.C. and the radio were powerful influences then. Hensor Morgan from Llangwm went home talking like Emlyn Williams after his first term in Trinity. His parents thought it was the Vicar at the door. Dai dropped no aitches. His consonants were beautifully articulated. His cadences and intonation, though, were too deep in his being for him to abandon those. He called us to attention now in immaculate Swansea-Oxford tones.

"Attention, gentlemen, please!" he sang. "Your efforts lack something. Let's see if we can find out what it is. Will someone kindly take my glasses? Thank you! And, now, will someone else point me towards the Buck." We weren't quite sure whether we should laugh at his self-deprecation and settled for giggling. Our generation still stood in awe of authority, even when it was friendly.

There was a moment's play as the man pretended to search for the Box. Then came the explosion of his energy. He launched himself down the Hall. He was on course for "even time" had he been running 100 yards. At his maximum speed, he hit the launching-pad, converting his forward momentum into height as he soared up and way over the Box. At exactly the right second and in perfect position, his hands and feet starred. His neck was arched, his head was back. High in the air, the angel was flying. He seemed to hover there as though suspended and then, with a fusion of force, his arms and legs went into "cut-off".

But we hadn't seen, and Dai Griff couldn't see, the inanimate object lurking there – as inanimate objects always do – waiting to intervene destructively in the affairs of the animate.

Mr. Griffiths had leapt so high into the air that the movable, horizontal beams, left slightly lower than their normal storage position in the ceiling, were in front of him as he drew up his knees and punched himself forward for landing. He smashed his forearms down on to the rounded, leading edge of the teak beam. At least ten feet above the floor, the vaulter became a falling angel. He crashed to the ground and lay there for a moment, during which none of us moved or muttered. Then, very slowly, he uncaffled himself, tendering his battered wings.

Sympathy for him was becoming mobile. People moved to help him. Still, none spoke until he did. Then, when he did, in a rather strangulated, standard English that had more rising and falling to the pitch of it than ever before, he said: "And that, gentlemen, was a blasphemous bloody silence!"

He wasn't bleeding. There was nothing to do with blood in that controlled oath, either, but the radius and the ulna in each of his forearms were chipped and cracked and, later, plastered at the hospital. In his performance that day, Dai Griff, in a failed vault, had leaped into our affections. We were his fans from that moment forward.

Captain Ithel Thomas, T.D., was probably younger than Dean Parry and God, but not much. "T.D." stood for Territorial Decoration. The captaincy probably related to the 1st World War, though he'd seen service in India and often referred to it during his lectures. Like the Dean, Ithel Thomas was very small and very bald. They were, indeed, physically, even facially, not unalike. The Captain, though, dressed in military style "civvies". He favoured "Winter Warms" and "Trench Coats", plaid shirts, green ties and flat caps, in matching Cheviot, with his twill-weave suits. His brown shoes shone like glass. Like many another ex-service man, the most memorable times of his life seemed to have been with "the Colours".

"In India", he would tell us, in physical geography lectures, "one was able to make a little money on the side because one knew a bit about meteorology and international weather patterns. I used to take wagers on when the rains would come. Bit unfair, really, because I'd learned not only the conditions that preceded the monsoons but that, on average, they came within a day or so of the same time each year."

One of his advanced-level geography students, I saw a fair amount of him. He was tutor-in-residence in the Wing more often than most, occupying the first study-bedroom on the ground floor to the right of its front doorway. During my second year, I lived next door to the tutor's room. At some time, I became his semi-official messenger. One of my duties was, weekly and, sometimes, more often, to collect money from him and to buy for him, on my trips into town, DuMaurier cigarettes in boxes of twenty.

Captain Thomas was active both in the College and in the town. Cecil Parry and I were active on College occasions. We came to be nominated by the Captain to move and to second votes of thanks to "gown" and to "town". Some of the events were prestigious and memorable and, since a small percentage of our final English marks were given for practical use of the language – as in College Chapel Bible readings – our appearances might have done us much good. Cecil's public speaking and mine were, in fact, mentioned favourably in my records and in his testimonial.

As interesting a character as any on the staff was Mr. John – "Johnny Humph" – Humphreys. He was the Vice-Principal, lectured in the principles and practice of education, supervised arrangements for and assessments of our teaching practices, and took a general interest in us.

A good lecturer, who made time fly when he talked, he never seemed in a hurry himself, nor was he particularly self-important, although he looked it with his stocky figure and expansive chest. In fact, he took his teaching more seriously than he took himself.

Johnny Humph was married to a doctor of medicine practising in Carmarthen. They had a daughter whose doings sometimes featured in her father's illustrations of points of psychology and patterns of child development. Growing up in a bilingual home, where both parents preferred to speak in Welsh but carefully rehearsed her in both languages, she featured in the interesting snippets that the fond father shared with us about his little daughter's linguistic development. "Daddy", she'd asked, "can you die in Welsh as well as in English?" Dead now, in both Welsh and English, Johnny Humphreys could hardly have thought that his daughter's question would be remembered and quoted fifty years on.

Mrs. Humphreys, Doctor Humphreys, was the College General Practitioner. She was also a lecturer in hygiene and health education, and shared the teaching of that with Dai Griff. She was in and out of the building all day, lecturing, diagnosing and prescribing. During our first year, a senior student – aptly named Shepherd – served as her assistant. Referred to as "Coll. Doc.", he made the rounds of the poorly to deliver their doses of medication as prescribed by Dr. Humphreys. He was also allowed to carry a thermometer and to take temperatures. His jurisdiction ended there. If temperatures rose or fell, he noted them and, if they rose or fell dramatically, he had to go to tell the tutor-in-residence or, failing his presence, report direct to the Principal. In my second year, I was "Coll. Doc." for a time.

Occasionally in life, we meet men or women who can't be measured by the mark that scores their contemporaries. Such a man was H. L. Harby. You've already met him. I've told you about his cryptic references to "pea-green copper joints" and to his supervision of the remodelling of the College structures. That man seemed able to do most things, and to do them well.

A lecturer in "Handwork", a generic title that covered working in wood, in metal, in cardboard and in any material that would serve us in acquiring useful skills for the classroom, he prepared his advanced-level students for examinations – practical and theoretical – that would qualify them to teach woodwork and metalwork up to Central Welsh Board Higher Certificate level. Part of their course involved making pieces of furniture in wood and intricate models in metals.

It was difficult to judge what his real love was. Along the way, he'd qualified as an architect. Over the last decade or so of Trinity's development, he had designed very substantial, innovative buildings. He had to his credit the creation of the Wing, the Broadcast Hall – now renamed in honour of Dean Parry – and the craft and other buildings on site. We were more than a little mesmerised by his competence and many talents, particularly since it seemed that the remodelling of the College Chapel was also credited to him.

This was made all the more amusing by his ironic attitude to the religious life of the College. He wasn't anti-clerical but he was a corrective to the sometimes too pervasive disciplines that hung-over from Dean Parry's days. The remarks weren't revolutionary but they were witty and welcome. He met me in the North Hall once on the morning of St. David's Day, affecting to be furious. Apparently, he'd been asked by the Principal to show a little more interest in the services in the chapel and to attend communion more regularly.

"Wouldn't you think", he asked, "that there'd be early communion on our Patron Saint's day? There isn't, you know. I set my alarm and got up at the crack of dawn, walked all the way over here, and there's no damn communion. I'll bet they'll have one on St. George's Day!" No-one, I think, made any greater contribution to the college than H. L. Harby.

His reputation, too, as had Dai Griff's, gained weight among us from an accident. Mr. Harby was showing his "Advanced" students how to use the circular bench-saw; a fiercesome electrical power-tool if ever there was one. "Treat it with respect", he warned. "All parts of the body always behind the guard on the cutting-edge. Feed the wood through with the push-stick. Always do it like this", and he made a perfect demonstration, cutting along the length of the moving plank, true to the end of the line.

The showman in him, the clear admiration of his audience, teased him on towards trouble though. "Always like that", he reiterated. "Never like this".

And he abandoned the push-stick, broke his own rule and – over-confident in his own competence – fed a new plank in by hand. The inanimate monster had been waiting for such a chance. Its spinning disc of razor teeth took H. L. Harby by the thumb and, in the split-second before the craft assistant had crashed the "Dead-man's handle" and halted the blade, it had bitten along the bone, through the knuckle, to the ball. There was blood everywhere except on Mr. Harby's face. He was, in the classic word, "rushed" to hospital. In a matter of days he was back. With his right hand strapped to his chest, he showed off, as though nothing much had happened, by writing on the blackboard with his left. We might have known that he'd be ambidextrous!

The Principal of King Alfred's College, Winchester, was an enigma of a man. Unlike the lean Handwork lecturer, he was a broad, robust chap out of the English middle-classes. Unlike Harby, he was a cleric. In fact, he was a Minor Canon of Winchester Cathedral and responsible, before moving to Carmarthen, for the cathedral music. He was Choir Master at Trinity, had a hand in teaching music alongside his history commitment, and lived in a set of College rooms up several flights of stairs not too far away from the Chapel; the only public schoolboy on a staff of self-propelled and state-educated meritocrats almost wholly from the working-classes.

An autocrat, intellectually arrogant, though not unfriendly, he was lecturing – having only just begun – when Barry Owen made a belated and fairly noisy entry to the room.

"Are you", asked the Rev. R. C. White – knowing full well that he was – "an historian?"

"Yes, Sir", said Barry. "I am."

White's expression feigned pain. "Then why enter the room with the appearance and demeanour of a rural scientist?" he asked as the sycophants fell about. Neither they nor he knew that he was clashing swords with a wit, intellect and memory well capable of squaring the circle.

There came a time, inevitably, when circumstances repeated

themselves. This time, on Barry Owen's very noticeable entry, Canon White stopped lecturing altogether. An interesting silence fell on the air, broken only by Barry's laying-out of his lecture notes, unscrewing the top of his fountain-pen. The silence continued after the student was ready, with the lecturer hamming up the situation as others began to giggle, but the biter was about to be bit. Slowly, E. Barry Owen reversed all his preparation. Capping his fountain pen, repacking his notes, he stood up again and made for the door.

"And where do you suppose you are going?" asked the cleric.

"I'm very sorry, Sir", said our Pembrokeshire boy with deadly politeness. "I made a mistake coming in here. I thought you were lecturing."

In fairness, R. C. White led the genuine laughter that rocked the room.

"If you'll sit down, Owen", he said, "I shall."

When I was very young – six or so – living in John Street, my brother – seven years older than I was – had told me to have nothing to do with a man who lived further up the street. "If you see him coming, you run", he said. I did, and I was all of fourteen-years-old before I found out why. I felt like taking to my heels again whenever I encountered Mr. White, and I encountered him often as a member of his Chapel choir and, in time, as Choral Secretary. I didn't really know why then, but I was uncomfortable in his presence. He dominated.

Early in our time at Trinity, some of us were invited into Principal White's study for what was advertised as a "sex education" lecture. Sex was always on my mind. Education was what I was at college for. Some two dozen of us crowded into the room. Mr. White presided from a fire-side chair. He spoke, perfectly properly, about the mechanisms and moralities of sex. After a while, he invited contributions "from the floor". The result was inevitable. Soon, we were into an adolescent competition to determine which amongst us were the most macho. A virgin, myself – though heterosexually ambitious – I was amazed where the seminar led us. I knew that every one from Pembrokeshire was a virgin, too, but these men from Glamorgan!

We were educated for more than an hour. Afterwards, on the way down the stairs, there was some reviewing of what it had all been about.

Charles Wilford has been introduced to you already. A mature man, probably into his fifties, tall and spare, pallid of complexion and stooping slightly, he contrived, rather cleverly, to let us know that he was on our side. His membership of the College staff was not the most important thing in his life, so he was not an establishment man. His main joy in life was his Model Practising School. His second – though the order could reverse itself from time to time – was his music. He loved teaching music at school and college, and he was good at it.

Music, during the first year of residence, was a compulsory subject. All of our year reported for it together in the large Examination Hall off the North Hall. Among us were genuine musicians. Some of them had instrumental qualifications already and were keen to add to them. These were the joy of Charlie's heart.

Sadly, they were buried deep in the dross of the rest of us. I wasn't the only one who, unsupported, couldn't hold a tune. Knowing that the only examination that we would face would be Mr. Wilford's in-house, end-of-term tests, we skived. There were more than seventy of us in the tutorial. Skiving was easy. The level of our learning was low. Charlie assumed that!

No concessions were made by this "man-among-children, child-among-men" enthusiast to the chronological age-range of his College students. His motto might well have been "Except ye become ... as little children" you shall not enter Charlie Wilford's academy of learning. Not only did he put the child in the place of "the original investigator", he insisted – more by example than precept – that the original investigator returned to his or her own origins in learning. Montessori and Kodail walked about wartime Trinity in the faded academic gown of its Model Practising School's headmaster.

You're familiar, I expect, with Kodail? He was the Hungarian who made the fingers "talk" to teach children the elements of music. Spreading fingers apart, pairing fingers together, relating one finger with others, and calling out their "given names", helped to make difficult concepts easier to grasp. "Ta", "Fa", "Ti", "Fe", "Ta-te" were, I seem to remember, Kodail's fingers and thumbs. Sadly, many of us were "all fingers and thumbs" in rehearsing his drills.

It was very funny, to see mature ex-servicemen try to force their fingers apart to do "Taf-a-tiffy-ta-te" in front of seventy of their barracking friends. Charlie Wilford would add to the fun by punching a note out of the piano with his fore-finger and then pointing the finger at someone who had to shout out its name in tonic solfa. Picked to answer, and without a clue, I prevaricated. "Me, Sir?" I asked. In asking the question, I'd inadvertently named the note. "Right, Sam", said Charlie, pleased, and moved on to a new victim. And then there was the moving of the piano.

The Examination Hall was used for more than examinations. A fine room, long and broad, lit by large windows, parquet-floored and high-ceilinged, it was in demand. As a result, its furniture was mobile, moved around to vary floor space. To make it easier to shift the Duck, Son and Pinker upright piano, the brass castors of which had, no doubt, been threatening the parquet, someone, probably H. L. Harby, had designed and turned four large, oak wheels – nine to ten inches in diameter – fitted them on axles, and mounted the piano on the axles.

"Fetch the piano, gentlemen", Charlie Wilf commanded at the beginning of a session one day. The piano was at the far end of the hall. Mr. Wilford, having failed to specify which gentlemen, had practically every one in the hall standing up. There was a race among many down the hall. Then, there was a struggle to grip the instrument. Men were bowled over, but a half-dozen or so grabbed the piano and set off with it at a run, knocking others sideways in the process. The music tutor – the model practised instructor – had the makings of a riot on his hands.

On the teaching dais, wrapped around in his gown, topped with his mortar-board, he fought for control.

"Stop!" he cried. "Stop where you are, this very minute!"

His command was effective. Every person in the hall clattered to attention, their thumbs coming to line with the seams of their trousers. They stood firm. But the piano was a freed spirit. Launched by a pack of strong young men, its lubricated axles and wooden wheels speeding it along, it was running free. Brushing aside chairs and tables, it ran and ran until finally, it arrived at the raised dais.

With the collision came the tempest of music. It would take Mr. Bolwel, the blind piano-tuner, days to drag it back into harmony after the storm of discord that jangled from it. Charlie would need some adjusting, too. He was more pallid than ever, as he tried to bring his lecture back out of hysterics.

He had a revenge of sorts. Announcing the Christmas examination results, he lined us all up, as he would the children at his school. Those whose marks were over 90% stood together in order of score. There were three of them. Those whose scores were in the 80% range – four people – lined up behind them. There were to be another five lines of scores called before "Sam" Parry came up.

I had heard Barry Owen humming the "sight reading" for my benefit during the exam. With that help, I topped the plus 10%ers and, as I took my place deep in the ranks but at the head of my line, someone with an even lower score shouted "Swot!"

So – as did Charlie Wilford, himself in all his teaching – we trod that line between being child-like and being childish. On either side and below that line were the pitfalls of the class-rooms and staff-rooms of the future.

John Rees, actually a goodish musician, was incensed. Used to being the right-hand marker on drill squares across Europe, he took very unkindly to being lined up for humiliation by a "civvy". "He'd better watch it", he said. "I might meet him in the dark."

Shortly afterwards, we went home for Christmas. That Christmas Eve, 3,000 allied planes "smashed" the French coast. Fortresses, Liberators and "medium bombers rocked special targets" and the R.A.F. "pounded Berlin with one thousand, one hundred and twenty tons of high explosives and fire missiles before dawn". General Eisenhower took command of preparations for D-day, and General Montgomery was named to head the British forces in the field. "God is Love?" "Peace in our time?"

It all seemed to put our first full term in Trinity back into perspective. With all that death and destruction about? "Tafa-tiffy-ta-te?" "Have a Merry Christmas!"

CHAPTER SIX

The Town

Believe it or not, wartime Carmarthen was an exciting place. I loved the town then and remember it with affection now. I pass close to it every week, by-passing it when driving out of Pembrokeshire on a Tuesday and back into it on a Thursday. Every time, I recall something of the days when I lived there.

We did live there, you see. We "went up" to College when term began. We "went down" at half-term and "back up" again a few days later. For more than six weeks at a time, the College was our home. We were involved in so much that we scarcely wanted to leave it for our own towns.

It's difficult, even for me, now, to understand that, almost within jogging distance of Neyland – only ten miles more than a marathon run away from it – I felt no compulsion to go there while the College was in session. Travel of any sort wasn't easy. Cash for railway and bus tickets was in short supply. Petrol was rationed. Private cars, except for sanctioned business trips, were virtually off the road, and my parents never owned a car in the whole of their lives. But it wasn't any of that. Quite simply, we had shifted the centre of our living.

As glad as the next man to go home when going home was on the agenda, and more than happy to take advantage of unexpected breaks, I certainly didn't suffer homesickness in between. There was no phone at our house, and none within a dozen houses of ours. I wrote home every week-end. I received a letter from home every Monday or Tuesday morning and, for the rest of the time, scarcely thought about home. Oh! Yes! I received a food parcel, together with my clean laundry, every week too, and sent my mother my dirty laundry in exchange.

There were some moments that were better than others and some that were downright difficult but, for most of the time, I couldn't get enough of the toing and froing, coming and going, and the exhilaration that I felt as a student in Carmarthen.

As I've hinted, the exhilaration had little to do with study. It was really about growing up, and Carmarthen, in 1943, was a good place in which to do that, when people only slightly older than we were had already been away – some of them thousands of miles away – from home already.

"A helluvaplace this Car-mar-then", exclaimed only the third American that I'd ever met. "There's a pub every other house, and a chapel every other pub!"

U.S. Servicemen – "the Yanks" – had that capacity to surprise. The Plaza Cinema, Neyland, had had us believing that the United States of America was Hollywood and that Hollywood was the United States of America. Each of the Americans – only three in all – that I had met up to the Autumn of 1943 had proved to be anything but Hollywood brash. We hadn't grasped properly, either, that all the southern United States citizens took a deep, historical objection to being mistaken for "Yankies".

My first meeting with a "Yank" had been in Neyland. That lad had looked Hollywood – sophisticated in his chocolate and cream uniform. It was tailored, pleated, belted and buckled. Each "permaglow" alloy button shone around the eagle that had landed on it. He was shiny-shoed, shirted, collared, tied and hatted, in a cut and style that only staff officers could aspire to in the British Army, and he was at the corner of John Street and Kensington Road, in Neyland, where we both waited to catch a bus to Milford. Born four thousand miles apart in distance – a Sabbath day's journey, at least, in cultures – and a little wary of one another, we were of an age. The American couldn't have been more than 19 years-old. He was a "General Issue" soldier: a "G.I." with no rank yet.

We had acknowledged one another and would have talked more but, just then, the double-decker bus – one of Green's newest and smartest – rounded Fred Rees's "Victoria House", turning from High Street into Kensington Road. It would stop opposite where we were, go on to George Street, and, reversing there, come back on our side of the road to pick us up.

The G.I. couldn't believe his eyes. You'd have thought that a new world had been created especially for him.

"Gee!" he gasped, elongating the vowels with a whole breathing lungful of air. "That's some bus!"

I'd lived with Green's Motors since childhood. "Don't you have double-deckers in America?" I asked.

"Is that what that is?" he queried. "One bus on top of another is a double-decker?" His up-and-down intonation, his double-vowelled accent, his almost Negroid emphases, I would have recognised later as coming from way down south of the Mason-Dixon line. He was from "Johnny Reb." country. His people would have fought the "god-damn Yankies".

"A double-decker", I confirmed. "You don't have them in the States?"

"The States", he'd answered, "is big country. I was only ever in one State for any time. Maybe we have double-deckers some place over there. Maybe they have great buses like that in New York. But we sure don't have 'em any place where I've been. A double-decker? That's some bus!"

We travelled together on it, on the upper deck, to Milford and, far from bragging about his own land, the lad was enchanted with my green country, with the blue sweep of the Cleddau estuary and with my Pembrokeshire Welsh down-below accent which, for him, "was real pretty English". We parted friends.

Within a week, I'd met my second American. Still, then, a sixth-former and crossing the Haven twice a day to and from school, I'd arrived at Hobb's Point, just missing one ferry and having to wait a quarter-of-an-hour for it to cross to the Neyland pontoon and return.

There was only one other seated on the long bench at the pier-head: a much older American soldier. His uniform was immaculate, new, though the clustered combat ribbons on it implied long service. So did his brindled hair. He wore a single brass bar on each shoulder epaulette. After I'd settled, exchanging time of day with him, he looked across at me.

"Boy", he said. "Will you get to go in the army?"

"Into one of the services", I said. I was a corporal in the Air Training Corps and the great ambition of my life, then, was to be a fighter pilot. "I'd like to join the R.A.F."

"If you do", he responded, "do me a favour?" His accent I recognised. I'd seen Jimmy Cagney, Pat O'Brien and John Garfield in "The Dead-End Kids". I knew that Bronx was pronounced "Bron-ix" and that New Yorkers crossed the "Willie-amsa-boiga Bridge", but how could I help? "What favour?" I asked.

"Will you remember what I'm tellin' you now? I was a Top Sergeant: a big, big fish in a small pond. Then, they gave me a commission. They made me a LOO-TENANT. Now, I'm a sardine in a great big ocean. If you get to be in your army, you'd best stay a non-commissioned officer, d'yu hear?"

I wonder what happened to him? Did he find a Field Marshal's baton in his knap-sack? Did he, like the side-board goldfish and Principal Halliwell, grow into his new dimension? Anyway, he taught me two things. The one was to look, beyond stereotyping, for the real people. The other was to appreciate what you have while you have it.

My third American had been as intrigued as I was with Carmarthen; the locked-away, Welsh-speaking market town – the oldest regional capital in Wales and walled outpost of the Romans in Demetia – that, suddenly, was open-house to a whole new army of charismatic strangers, living on its doorstep in a city of huts with a population many times its own. What a drama that was! Almost overnight, the biggest culture shock since the Norman occupation of West Wales had set the echoes ringing under the ruins of the castle and broken defences of those earlier invaders. Back in America – "States-side" – homework had been done.

Lammas Street was new to us. We were exploring the broad, main highway from Picton's Monument to Nott's Square and the shops that opened off its pavements, when we were hailed by an enormous "Yank". As big and strong as anybody that I'd ever seen, towering over the dylanesque, average height of the Welsh men and women around him, this senior warrant officer, in combat dress, held a tiny phrase-book in the palm of one hand. The forefinger of the other hand was pointed at a page and keeping the book open.

"Prynhawn da, cockies!" he bawled, in a Welsh accent at least as good as mine. "Ma'en – braf iawn. Ydych ein siarad – Saesneg?" There were pauses between words as he stitched them together but Gwynfor Evans would have applauded his effort.

"Yes, we do", we said. From Pembrokeshire, all four of us, we spoke little else. We had a certificate each, attesting to our "Oral proficiency" in French, 600 years after those Norman conquerors had been absorbed and their castle ruined, but here was a newly landed, temporary immigrant making a better effort with our mother tongue than ever our mothers' tongues had done in not teaching it to us. That was the way of it in Wales then.

The warrant officer seemed more disappointed than pleased that he could now speak without his phrase-book. "We had lessons in Welsh", he said, pronouncing it "Wal-ish". "They said you guys all spoke it. Why don't you?"

Why indeed? It would have taken some explaining. Our instinct would have been to move on, but we weren't going to be allowed to do so. The meeting had convened outside Conti's. "Say! Why don't we all grab a coffee? I want to ask you lots an' lots about your great little city," said this gracious visitor. There was much that we could ask him. We went in.

Conti's was then run in the absence of adult, male Contis. That lovely Carmarthen family of long-settled Italian immigrants became "enemy aliens" overnight when, on 10th June, 1940, with German armoured forces running riot around the defences of France and only four days away from capturing Paris, Il Duce, Benito Mussolini, judged it to be time to join the "winning" side, and Italy declared war on Britain and France. That morning, the family had been awakened by a stone crashing through the café window. They and the other Welsh Italians, many from the mountain village of Barci – the Rabbaiottis, the Sidolis, the Saccadelis, the Bassinis, the Fortés – who, as Wales became a steam-coal centre of Western Europe's industrial revolution, had been drawn in, to service the high streets of developing Welsh towns with espresso, capuccino and sweet, dark, scalding, "regular" coffee, offering with it an immaculate service in the best of food and fruit drinks, were no longer to be trusted to walk the pavements of the towns they'd thought were home. They'd gone to bed "Welsh-Italians". They awoke "enemy aliens".

As we and our friendly ally entered their café, they languished in the mists of Mannanan, in a concentration camp on the Isle of Man. For almost every one of them, their incarceration had been a travesty of justice. War brings out man's latent inhumanity to man, and encourages the stupidities of broad-brush bureaucracy.

Years later, Angelo Conti and I were recuperating from accidents, mending broken bones in the Glangwili hospital that was to be the last benefice to West Wales from the U.S. Army's friendly occupation of Carmarthen and a lasting monument to the presence of the 12th U.S. Evacuation Hospital Corps and of the 232nd Station Hospital Corps in and around the town in the 1940s. He told me of the pain and bitterness of that other accident of war. His "a reverderci Roma: bore da Caerfyrddin" cadences, accentuated – twenty years on – the brutalisation of the feelings of a little boy lost.

"I went to bed 'appy, a Carmarthen school kid. Next morning, I 'eard a crash. Then, I 'eard my mother cryin'. When I ran into their room, my father was at the window. He was cryin', too, lookin' down into the street. Down there were our neighbours. The day before, they'd been our friends. One of them had put the brick through the café window. They were cryin' as well – cryin' out for our imprisonment.

"In one night, only, this Welsh boy had become a "W.O.P." In one night, only, our friends had become our enemies. I've never trusted anyone since!"

Maybe for as long as a thousand years – for the next millennium – Serbs, Croats, Bosnians, of all faiths and of none, will trust no-one in the world either.

Unaware or unheeding of that family's misery within the greater sorrow of war, we drank coffee and ate doughnuts at the expense of our ally in the enemy aliens' café. That day, we would probably have called Angelo a "W.O.P.", too. In wartime, propaganda is truth, and truth is one of the first casualties of war.

After the coffee and doughnuts, we roamed the main streets of Carmarthen together. Later in the year, our route would have become automatic. That day, we were wandering. We took in the shops, lingered in Woolworths, examining the good things on and behind the counters. Nott's Square was an up-one-side-and-down-the-other perambulation. The Shire Hall, with its County Court and Borough Council offices, sat at one end of the square, taking up a great deal of space. A balcony and a building-long frontage of steps faced out on the square.

There was a square beyond the square. Since it was a market town, principally serving farmers and the people who lived off them, the shops dealt in quality goods. There was a particularly fine choice of tailoring and haberdashery shops. General and ironmongery stores abounded, and there were restaurants and cafés in almost every street.

As our tame American had said – stretching things a bit – there seemed to be a great many public-houses and more than a few chapels. Not "a pub every other house and a chapel every other pub", but a generous placing of both.

Our Top-Sergeant, First Class, had turned out to be an academic himself, "graduating" – though the word might have gained something in translation – from a State College and "majoring" in education.

Since, soon, it was towards evening and we were due back at Trinity for supper – which we were learning to call dinner – we took him with us, intending nothing much more than touring him round the place and showing him off to our friends. He was to enjoy much more than that. As we made our rounds, this bulky and gregarious man attracted a great deal of attention. In no time, he was being lionised. Seniors told him of their uncles who'd been off to Philadelphia in the morning. Others claimed kinship with ex-Presidents of the U.S.A. At some point, he was shanghaied by the staff, by Dai Griff and 'Llew" Llewellyn, and moved out of our orbit. When we saw him next, we were all on our feet for grace in the Dining Hall, and our splendid Yank was towering between Principal Halliwell and Vice Principal Humphreys like a Californian Yoshemite Redwood planted in an apple orchard in Wales.

For a while, he would visit the college, occasionally. We gained status as "the ones who brought him here". He gained status as the first Yank at the court of St. David, or at least at the diocese's premier training college. The Principal gained status from hosting the first American soldier to dine – in that particular war – at Trinity College, Carmarthen. It had been a good day for most of us who were not Welsh Italians.

Soon, our excursions into town were taking a regular pattern. We walked there. There was no virtue in that. There was no alternative other than the bicycle, and it surprises me now that I don't remember many riding one, either within the grounds or back and fore to town. As for cars – which had to be immobilised, anyway, by the removal of the rotor-arm from the carburettor when parked – there were only two or three of those around the place, and they usually belonged to visitors: never to students. So, we walked into town and back.

I suppose it rained, often. The wind must have blown. Those are not the Carmarthen town days that I remember. Clear in my mind are those sun-shine afternoons when the sky was blue, when the clouds were small, white, flat underneath, rounded on the top and mobile, and when our anticipation was matched with realisation. We were going to do – and we did – wonderful things, like walking round the mart, looking at farmers and their animals, while farmers and their animals looked at us, in our tricolour Trinity scarves and ties, flaunting our new badges of honour. We didn't actually have blazers or badges. They cost too much.

The mart, then, was at the heart of Carmarthen, physically, commercially, and in every other sense. We could smell it from a mile off. We could hear it from further away: the lowing of the cattle, the cows separated from their calves, and the calves who clamoured for their mothers. Sheep would be calling. Pigs would be squealing. As we drew nearer, great clouds of horse-flies would be rising and falling where giant Shire horses, broad Welsh Cobs and short mountain ponies stamped and whinnied. Then there were the cockerels crowing, the hens squawking and the feathers flying, and the dung, the droppings, and the pee that pooled and stank the place.

What a splendour of plumage and cacophony of cackling the poultry made. Chickens, in those days, went walkabout with their clothes on, unless they were already in the hands of the butchers and bare. So, there were magnificent birds, in full feather, to admire. Their names were magnificent, too: White Wyandottes, Blue Leghorns, Buff Orpingtons, Rhode Island Reds, all in the fine feathers that made them such fine birds. Where did they come from, these exotic creatures? Well, in the short-term, from places with even more exotic names. From Gwili and Abergwili, from Ffynnonddrain and Bronwydd, from Cynwyl Elfed, Horeb, Hermon, Brechfa, they came in their unborrowed plumage to be bought and sold in the open pens alongside the Capitol Cinema. The cocks crowed as though St. Peter was about, and lambs for the slaughter passed us by on the road as if it were all on an April evening rather than a September afternoon.

"Scrapie" in adult sheep was known but disregarded as a human hazard. Bovine Spongiform encephalitis – hazard, hysteria, or not – was half a century away.

So, Carmarthen was, then, unashamedly carnivorous. So were most of us. Vegetarians were thin on the ground. Humanitarians, in a "world" war, didn't hold centre-stage. This mart was a bloody battleground, too: a little holocaust of its own. What a hypocrite I would be if I pretended that I knew that then and cared. A carnivorous Saul of Tarsus, and unconverted to vegetarianism to this day, I was "consenting unto the death" of these martyrs to our appetites.

My father had been born a hill-farmer, high in the rounded hills on the Welsh side of Kilvert Country. His people had worked thin soil on the higher ground above Painscastle, Builth and

Llandrindod since before records were kept. At Molleston, my mother had raised chickens, and my father pigs. At Neyland, in wartime, pigs and chickens, reared in back yards, supplemented rations and became a form of currency as sections of illicit corpses were handed over back-garden walls in the "black-out", and half-pigs were thrown, in the moonlight, through open windows, into welcoming hands. Preferring our vegetation recycled into more solid food, we were certainly not unhappy in the farming market-place. It was life and death as we lived it then, and the slaughter-house was an adjunct to the farmhouse. Veal was veal. The pretty little calves with their liquid eyes were for patting – petting, even – in passing. Their destination wasn't discussed.

Currency – pounds, shillings and pence, sterling – was rather a problem. In my weekly letter from home, I received a Postal Order. It was for five shillings, and intended to fund all of my extra-mural activities for the week. It's almost impossible to effect an accurate comparison. In "new" money, what would you need for two days out a week in Carmarthen? In old money, we knew exactly what we could get.

We could get a free look around the mart. Another splendid free showroom waited in the market – wet or dry – under the high roof of the modern, metal Market Hall. Looking in shop windows, merrying around our favourite route about town, cost nothing. There was even a popular song out of Hollywood to cheer us on our way: "The best things in life are free". D'you know, I don't think I knew that I was poor then. Perhaps you don't, until somebody tells you. As for that modern disease of adolescence, being "bored", the word wasn't in our vocabulary. There was just too much to do, to see, to taste, to touch, to smell and to hear that cost us nothing. Poor? Bored? Not on your Carmarthen wartime life!

But the colour, the confusion, the bilingual babble, the surging up of smells, the teasing taste of market tea strong in the air, the fish stall, and the fly-swats and fly-papers – hanging with the black bodies of the swarms that had gone to their sticky doom preserved in arsenic – made the day.

There was so much mess about. Neither the market nor the mart was a place for the fastidious to put their feet down carelessly. There were pushing and shoving, but there were colour and light and sights and sounds in the best free show in town before we surrendered our first twelve pence for tea and two slices of buttered toast in a café opposite the Lyric. We knew how to live and – glory be to God! – we were alive and living when there was a lot of dying about.

Wednesday, after Harriers, was cinema day. Out of my five-shilling Postal Order, I had to hold back the price of a seat, in the Capitol or the Lyric. I seem to remember that the cheapest seats, right up at the front, under the screen, cost as little as six pence for the Wednesday or Saturday afternoon matinée. For nine pence, you could sit further back, with a less oblique view and undistorted sound. I believe that we paid one shilling, if we'd budgeted well. There were special, courting seats in one of the cinemas – I forget which – that accommodated two people, side-by-side, with no seat arm intervening between them. They cost as much as half-a-crown apiece. On our sort of funding, if we'd aspired to one of those, it would have been essential to meet the girl inside.

Do I need to try to recapture for you the magic and the mystery of cinema in the thirties and forties? Generations brought up on television – viewing TV alone in an upstairs room or downstairs in the family ambit, with home-life going on around the edges – could scarcely make the transit, now, to the glory days of the "silver screen".

William Connor, the famous "Cassandra" of the *Daily Mirror*, captured the difference – encapsulated it for me – in one of his brilliant post-war columns. He regretted that television hadn't been invented before cinema. "Imagine", he wrote – or words to that effect – "the excitement there would be if a generation conditioned to watching people six inches tall moving about on a silly little screen only twenty-one inches high were to be told that in an especially designed, superbly comfortable theatre, they could go to see all their heroes performing, not only life-size but larger than life? Wouldn't they flock there in droves to see such a wonder?"

Television had been invented long before the war but was available to the very few, very rich, and I hadn't even seen a television set in 1943. Free of it, we flocked in droves to see such wonders as the cinema brought to us and led us into.

"What a pity", my father said, "that the churches and chapels allowed Hollywood to get into the clutches of the devil!" He was in the pulpit when he said it. He preached to good numbers in his congregation but he'd realised already that the communication of the future would be through moving pictures – "walkies" and "talkies" – and believed that the pervasive, new medium was by-passing obsolescent sermon-services with formidable impact and "inferior" messages. The cinema was, in almost every sense, more comfortable than the chapel.

Seeing that his experience of cinema was limited – he and my mother saw their first silent film on a one-day honeymoon to Barry Island in 1915, and only very rarely saw others – his judgement of the power and influence of film, biased though it was and sectarian, could hardly be faulted.

We were taken out of ourselves once, and, with luck, twice, a week in the comfy dark of the matinée. Sometimes it was the cuddly, comfy dark. For two or three hours we walked on other planets; we were other men. We won the war with John Wayne before the war was won. We walked the roads to Rio and to Morocco behind the undulating behind of Miss Dorothy Lamour in lands of Hope and Crosby. We scandalised civil war-torn Atlanta, Georgia, with Clark Gable and Vivienne Leigh and, even if we had suspected that my father's judgement was right, there, in that insidious luxury of escapism, "frankly" we didn't "give a damn".

On this business of Carmarthen and its pubs and chapels, I'm a lopsided witness. Curiously, all of my immediate group of friends were, at the time, teetotal. The Pembrokeshire contingent wasn't into the pub culture. Indeed, I never tasted alcohol, wittingly, until I was 43-years-old and afraid to drink the water on a caravanning holiday in France. It didn't seem to me that there was too much hard drinking done by many of our contemporaries either.

Those who did drink swore by the "White Horse". Dai Griff, they said, swore by it, too. His reasons, though, were more complex than theirs. He loved the landlord's daughter and married that very lovely girl.

Although College Chapel attendance was compulsory for certain services, and I was drawn into others as a member of the choir, I also attended the Baptist Chapel in town. The Rev. Mr. Prothero presided there. Later, his son, Alan, a baby then, was to become a good friend of mine when he was a senior figure in the B.B.C. at Broadcasting House.

I remember, too, reciting "I vow to thee, my country, all earthly things above, entire and whole and perfect, the service of my love" at a special chapel "rally" of all the youth organisations of the town.

The town and chapel giant, though, was without question "The Black Prince". He wasn't black. He wasn't a prince. Mr. D. J. Evans was, I believe, a solicitor's clerk, but he didn't look like one, and it was easy to see why he'd been nicknamed. A big man for a Welshman, he had almost all the other typical features of our race. Broad-shouldered, short but thick in the neck, barrel-chested, he was dark-haired – combing back a shock of it – and Celtic-dark in complexion. An important man, he dressed importantly. His clothes were pre-utility. The lapels of his jacket were generous. His trousers "turned-up" in classical style. His waistcoat and watch-chain measured and anchored his middle, but the surest signs of his importance were his silk cravat, his large, pearl cravat-pin, and the turned-back wings of his shirt collar. Starched stiff, protuberant, they framed and supported his square jaw. Did the Celts, on their westward journey, pass through Serbo-Croatia? That's where the cravat fashion came from. The word was a corruption of the Croat "Hravat", the neck-scarf worn by Croat mercenaries in the French Army during the Thirty Years War. Short of a war of their own, they rented out their truculence.

The "Black Prince" might well have been a Balkan aristocrat or a tamed brigand sent to make diplomatic rings around international negotiators for peace in any one of the wars that Serbs and Croats have been fighting all my life, but he was not. He was a Baptist, a Christian, a chapel secretary, and – above all – he was the genius and driving-force behind Carmarthen's most astonishing cultural society: the Young Men's Debating Society. No-one who was anyone refused an invitation to speak to the Society. D. J. Evans's request was a royal command. Carmarthen town benefited from what might well have been the widest and deepest public education programme that any unofficial, provincially-based group has ever mounted in Wales.

During our relatively short time in that small market town, we were part of the packed chapel audience – many, many hundreds crowded in – to hear on different occasions Archbishop Fisher of Canterbury; the "Red Dean", Dr. Hewlett Johnson; the Stipendiary Magistrate for East London and former student of Trinity, Mr. Daniel Hopkin; Mr. Hopkin Morris, the Liberal M.P.

for Carmarthen, and his Party Leader, Mr. Clement Davies, Q.C., M.P. Sir Stafford Cripps, later to be Labour's austerity Chancellor of Exchequer, lectured sternly there, too.

On one epic occasion, we managed places in the gallery when hundreds had to sit in the "overflow" meeting in the schoolroom, to hear a tall, lean, elderly man, with almost querulous delivery down a prominent nose, tell of his revolutionary plan, produced a year earlier, for social justice in post-war Britain. He was the ascetic, brilliant Sir William Beveridge. However quavering the voice and lofty the tone, the substance was electrifying. No Revival congregation could have thrilled to a preacher more than that audience did to Beveridge as he made the statistical and financial bases to his plan – and the inevitability of its adoption by any future British government – seem understandable, logical and desirable.

The '44 "Butler" Education Act, too, was introduced to the immensely privileged Young Men's Society and its guests by Professor Green, Professor of Education at University College of Wales, Aberystwyth. Not only did it guarantee the "three M's", which were "Meals, Milk and Money to provide them" but it introduced "the three A's" in the biggest step forward in public education since 1900. "Butler's" Bill would usher in "the three A's" by making it the duty of local government, requiring it to provide, free of cost to the pupil or student, whatever education proved relevant to the "Age, Aptitude and Ability" of the individual, regardless of race or religion or anything else. The use of the power to "require" Britain's Local Education Authorities to implement the Bill when it became an Act was the major step forward. Pre-war education had been a patchwork of provision: a lottery. Where you lived determined what you received. Opportunity was to exist nation-wide.

Come back, R. A. Butler! If only, today, we could move forward to 1944! The optimism of those great meetings when, in the dark days of war, our country was planning a better, fairer, more integrated society for its people in peace, and meeting-halls and chapels were crowded to the door with those who wanted to hear about it all, contrasts starkly with the pessimism, the cynicism, the lonely individualism, that keep people apart and ensure, it seems, the election and re-election of the politics of greed. We were designed to stand on our own feet, but on the ground, not on the shoulders of the less fortunate: nor does it serve a democracy when its politics and its politicians, regardless of party, are not heard with respect by the bulk of the people.

In 1943 – or, maybe, 1944 – politics were so much a part of Carmarthen town, and our democracy was so confident, that the British Communist Party in Wales rented the Capitol Cinema and advertised a public meeting for a Sunday evening. It was the "Stalingrad Sword" sort of period. The invasion of Russia by Germany had been turned, defeated by the heroism and "burnt earth" defences of the Russians, by the Russian winter, and by the opening of the "2nd Front" and allied bombing of German cities and industrial complexes. The people of Britain would mark their respect for the living and the dead defenders of Stalingrad by having a Sheffield-steel sword forged for presentation to the City.

We learned that Harry Pollitt, the General Secretary of the British Communist Party, was to speak; supported by the Rev. Bryn Thomas, the Christian-communist vicar of the parish of Kemble, in Gloucestershire. Cecil Parry and I decided to go to hear them. Can you imagine a Carmarthen cinema today overcrowded by a Communist Party meeting? The Capitol was, that night. Comfortably seated ourselves, we enjoyed the pre-meeting fuss and fun among the noisy crowd. When the curtains went back, I had the shock of my life. The meeting's Chairman was my Uncle Evan from Betws Road, Betws, Ammanford; a miner's agent in the West Wales coalfields.

Evan Evans, according to family legend, had travelled from Trefil to Llanelli for little more than a day out as a young teenager. He'd extended the trip, at the suggestion of a travelling companion who had relatives in Ammanford. In the best of "Penny Romance" tradition, he'd met the girl of his life there and, effectively, left home there and then. My mother's eldest brother and one of my father's best friends, his politics were as uncompromising as my Dad's religious faith, and their respect was mutual.

Once, my father had warned one of his deacons off tangling with his brother-in-law in the dialectics of Christianity and Communism. "Unless you know as much about Marx as Ianto knows about Matthew, I should leave him alone", he'd cautioned.

Known in our family as Ianto and, in the ferocious politics of coal production as "Ianto Bolshie", he had helped Arthur Horner and others to found and to consolidate the mine-workers' union in Wales. He was so adamantly "Left" that the immensely respected James Griffiths was a "Shoni bob-ochor" to him, and that other ex-miner hero of socialism, Aneurin Bevan, was a "deviationist".

A gigantic intelligence, starved of formal education, avid for learning: an energy almost too great to be contained in the athletic, above-six-foot frame and broad shoulders of the lad who'd cut coal since his fourteenth birthday, and a brooding, pale, saturnine but handsome man, Evan was a prisoner of no-one's conscience but his own. The same James Griffiths – a hero of mine – once told me: "If Ifan had known how to compromise, he could have been in the Cabinet, too".

But he didn't. He hadn't. And there he was introducing, to a huge and not unfriendly audience, "the next Prime Minister of Britain, Comrade Harry Pollitt". Comrade Pollitt was in good form. "The Comrade Vicar of Kemble in Gloucestershire" was in better. Both articulated the triumphs of the "peace-loving people of the U.S.S.R." against the "Nazi, fascist, war-machine". It was by any standards – heckles, questions and all – a great meeting. There were two Communist members of Parliament already – Willie Gallacher and Phil Pirattin. Conceivably, after a meeting like that in Liberal country like Carmarthen, there could be more. Neither Cecil nor I really believed that Harry Pollitt would ever be Prime Minster but – going down to the stage as the meeting ended to greet and to congratulate Uncle Evan, who was delighted to see "My youngest sister's boy" and introduce us to his co-speakers – we didn't say so.

Later, we walked back from town to college in the darkness, mulling over what we had heard and seen. At that time, Cecil was, perhaps, more interested in the politics of it than I was. Both of us, though, had been enchanted by the vibrancy, the commitment and the captivating challenge of it all. Democracy was good stuff when it gave all men a platform!

While we, two eighteen-year-olds from Pembrokeshire, walked through the dark up the graded hill to Trinity, another Pembrokeshire lad who, only months before, had been a student at the College, with his room in the Wing, was walking back to Boncath.

"What is that?" you might ask. "What has that to do with anything?"

It has a great deal to do with everything about those tangled, upside-down, back-to-front years of 1943-'44 and '45, and the havoc and the horror and the humour – the consequences and the inconsequentialities – of Western Europe at war.

You remember my mentioning that Christmas Eve air bombardment of those continental targets, when the French coastal ports had been "smashed", and Berlin had been "pounded" with "one thousand, one hundred and twenty tons of high explosives and fire missiles before dawn" on Christmas Day? That all happened in only one night of Allied, British-based, Bomber Command's early-forties onslaught on "Fortress Europe". We know now, we didn't then, that it was coming to its peak in effort, output, heroism and slaughter during our first Spring Term at Trinity. Under the onslaught, 600,000 people died in Germany alone. 55,573 British and Commonwealth air-crew died in sustaining the attacks. No-one of those airmen would have been older than the oldest student, then, with us in College. Some would have been almost as young as the youngest of us. One of them had left Trinity only three months before the two Parrys had arrived there. That Pembrokeshire lad's transition from H. L. Harby's Flight of the Swansea University Air Squadron had – in less than a year – taken him into high-flying adventure, tumbling danger, and trauma.

James Arthur Davies – 1615898, Flight Sergeant Davies, J.A. – walking back to Boncath, as we walked back to Trinity, through the dark – was barely 20-years-old that night. Yet, twice already, he had made "the long journey from Ludford to Berlin". And the second of his journeys had ended with a leap in the dark.

"Jim" Davies, of Bryn-Hedydd, Boncath, Pembrokeshire, had been, as he says, "oblivious of the drama" building up aboard Lancaster bomber D.V.267 – code-named "K for King" – because of his special duties amidship, manning innovative radio, "scrambling" programmes to confuse ground defences. Over the target, his particular duty done, he'd become "aware of the very real, immediate and desperately urgent situation" all around him.

"The crew were already at their Prepare to Abandon positions in the aircraft and were preparing to leave, waiting for the final command. The plane was now burning furiously. There was a sickly smell of cordite."

It's not for me, is it? to intrude too far into the tale that our long-ago lad and living legend recalls for himself and for us so vividly in his book, "A Leap in the Dark", but it is relevant to this one of mine that, after "falling very rapidly into a black sky" on leaping, and uttering an extempore prayer in Welsh, which was both a plea for help and a veiled threat – "Ein Tad, dyma dy gyfle Di'" – he'd pulled the rip-cord of his parachute, floated down, and made "a spectacular landing in a small canal between the meadows covered by a thin veneer of ice".

The immediate past-student of Trinity, the future Trinity College, Carmarthen, lecturer; Pembrokeshire County Education Authority Deputy Director; and, ultimately, Principal Dr. J. A. Davies, of The Normal College, Bangor, could have been readily forgiven if he'd sat down then, where he was, 50 miles into Nazi-occupied Holland from its border with Germany. He might, easily, have waited – bruised and beaten as he'd been – to be picked up and interned. He would have been protected by the sanctions of the Geneva Convention. His war could have ended, there and then. Many, far from home, alone, frightened, might have settled for that. Not our Jim!

He picked himself up off the fractured ice, in the foreign darkness. He stripped off his parachute harness, his scorched flying-suit and any identifiable R.A.F. clothing. One flying-boot already lost in baling out, he abandoned the other. Now, he stood garbed in an overall that would not call attention to itself anywhere in Europe. He'd been wearing "comforter" slippers over his socks in his flying-suit. All that he was not now wearing he bundled together, having first retrieved survival packages, "iron" rations and currencies, compasses, and maps-on-silk provided in the standard kit. He stowed all the other evidence of his landing deep in the canal side. "It was", he says, "a quarter-to-three in the morning of 20th February, 1944. It was Sunday morning and bitterly cold."

In little better than stockinged-feet, James Arthur Davies set his compass to the stars and began walking back to Boncath. The walk was to take him almost all of the time that we were to be at Trinity.

There were, after all, more dangerously exciting places than Carmarthen for teenagers from Pembrokeshire in that wartime winter of 1944.

The College Choir, with choirmaster, the Rev. R. C. White, Principal of King Alfred's College, Winchester.

CHAPTER SEVEN

The Choir

My membership of the choir – my selection for it – is something of a mystery still. The mechanics of selection are not. They were arbitrary. As we sang in College Chapel in our earliest services there, the predator, "Prinny" White, prowled the pews. He listened to the singers and did a little tap-tap on the shoulder of anyone with a voice that he liked. Having been tapped, you were on your way to being chosen. I was tapped and presented myself later, in the ante-chapel, for further auditioning. None took place. I was told that I'd been selected.

Eric Orsman was auditioned. R. C. White commanded him to sing the scale. Quiet though he was by nature, Eric was not easily dragooned. He sang "Doh! Ray! Me! Fa! So! La! Te! Doh!" all on the same flat note, without variation in pitch from first to last. The Minor Canon looked hard at him. "Are you tone deaf?" he asked. "Yes, Sir, I think so", said our lad. "So do I", responded the Choir Master, and Eric Orsman had escaped, to sing when he wanted to, not on command. His early victory over the disestablished Church must have strengthened his confidence. He married a vicar's daughter.

But I joined the choir. My years of sprinting down our back-lane had taught me that I was faster over a hundred yards than "Cinders" Brown, and I was fitter now than I'd ever been. Some of the choristers were long, strong and ugly, men with mean muscles, even though their voices were angelic, and I relaxed into total enjoyment of the fine-tuning that our choral-master gave to the undoubted musical ability of the majority. There were as many good musicians as good voices in that choir and – supported on either side by better men – I became a tenor.

There were advantages and disadvantages to singing in the choir.

First among disadvantages was having to get up earlier on Sundays and Saints' days. There were, also, the weekly choir practices of an hour or so: anthems to learn, Eucharists to sing.

The great advantage was rehearsing and getting to know hymns that might not have featured in the Baptist Church Hymnal or the "1,200 Sacred Songs and Solos" of I. D. Sankey and W. S. Moody. I have a confession to make. Not only do I not – even yet – hold a tune with confidence but I don't really get much inspiration from music in itself. My admitted addiction is to words. The timbre, the rhythm, the rhyming, the alliteration, the assonance, the sound, the echo, and the sense of words – spoken, written or sung – have always been enough. Sankey and Moody, the Salvation Army and Johnny Cash have the balance about right for me. I love the lyrics as much, if not more, than the music.

Yes! I know what Shakespeare said in "The Merchant of Venice"!

> "The man that hath no music in himself,
> Nor is not moved with concord of sweet sounds
> Is fit for treasons, stratagems, and spoils;
> The motions of his spirit are dull as night,
> And his affections dark as Erebus:
> Let no such man be trusted."

"Not guilty!" I plead. "Not true!" I argue. There is music in me. My problem lies in the way tunes come out of me. I'm spastic in tune-holding. But I'm totally moved "with concord of sweet sounds"; for me the sweet sounds of the human voice don't always need accompaniment. Even Shakespeare's plays can be ruined by that curse of stage, radio and screen, obtrusive "background" music, crashing away, irrelevantly, in the foreground.

"Treasons, stratagems, and spoils", or not, I hope to be trusted because the motions of my spirit – even in advanced old age – are absolutely not as "dull as night". They are, as they have always been, star-struck, moon-lit, sun-kissed; day-lit from within and without by the joy of waking up every morning and by a sense of wonder at the privilege of being a part of whatever is going on in my particular bit of the world.

There's another thing. Learning by rote was – disastrously – dropped from the schools' curriculum in the 50s and 60s: largely, I suspect, under pressure from schools' inspectors and "with-it" teachers who hadn't been good at committing things to memory themselves. Earlier, the Sunday Schools had died away. Competition, in day school or anywhere else, became politically incorrect. Later, school eisteddfodau were crowded out with so much else by the National Curriculum. In every way, whatever came in, growing children were the losers, from what went out.

When is someone going to build the processes, if not the systems, back? Singing in the choir reinforced my memory. Words that rhymed, lines that scanned, rhythms that ran, set to good tunes, helped me and generations of us to build up a bank in our brains from which we could draw dividends every day of our lives.

Real blank verse – not someone's inferior prose cut up into unequally sliced lines and presented as poetry – wasn't difficult to hold in mind, either. The Psalms, the hymns – "Ancient and Modern" – the towering structures of the "Authorised Version" and the glory and the innuendo of the Apocrypha – the riot of love, lust and sex, softened by romance set to the harp, in the Song of Solomon, balanced by the corrective disciplines of the Book of Common Prayer, were reinforced for me or introduced to me in all the services that I attended when singing with the choir. It all had a touch more of pomp and ceremony than your average Sankey service in the Mission Hall, Hazelbeach, but I was fairly pompous myself and drawn to the ceremonial, and there was blessed irreverence to relieve the tension, if it all became a bit heavy.

"Let us pray!" sang the Precentor.

"O.K.!" responded half the choir, under the cover of "The Lord's name be praised!" of the other half, who were trying not to grin, with their eyes shut.

Students, you'll remember, were expected to read lessons chosen for them by the Rev. R. C. White, who also allocated them marks for their readings. After each such chapel reading, he also pinned a "crit" of the performance on the notice-board in the Cloisters for anyone who was interested to read. Our Minor Canon also seemed to have a sense of malicious humour. A friend of ours, from the Amman Valley, testified to it.

The names of chosen readers were also displayed on the Cloisters' notice-board, together with names of the Books of the Bible and the chapter and verses they were to read. In what might have been an error but was, probably, a practical joke, Evan's verses ran to the end of one chapter and were clearly intended to run over into the next. For that day, the instructions had been unclear.

Reading from the Chapel lectern was an ordeal. Most people recoiled from doing it. Everyone was glad to get it over. Some of the swiftest scripture readings in history must have been made at that lectern. Even those that began in measured tones and lower registers accelerated and moved from baritone to tenor and – in extreme cases – to castrato, as important muscles in the throat, thorax and scrotum strangulated through fear.

Evan's was a better effort than most, but a pit had been dug for him. His voice was naturally deep and stayed down, even as he sped towards his last verse. "AND", he read, "WITH MY WHOLE HEART I SAID: ... HERE ENDETH THE FIRST READING."

Whether of his performance or of someone else's – cruelly undermining the soaring sopranos of lesser men – the notice-board "crit" once stated: "The reader read in a rich, basso-profundo voice, than which there is none other more beautiful". We were a part of a pedantry, up with which we had to put, and R. C. White was a bass baritone.

Actually, the Chapel was beautiful. Unusually, I believe, it faced south, taking its morning light from the south-west. In service and out of it, the chapel atmosphere was tranquil. Its lean lines led the eye forward to the chancel and the high altar. Its furniture, its fittings, the honeyed sandstone of its walls, were spare, without asperity, and free of any sense of austerity. There were fawns and there were whites and the warm, mellow woodwork of the pews. Light and borrowed colours spilled, later in the day, into the place from the eastern wall windows and, against opposing buttresses to the arch of the chancel, stood the pulpit on the one hand and the lectern on the other, prominent against the white walls. The arch was a drawn-back stone curtain, framing the stage above the chancel steps where – at an altar faithful to the proportions of the chapel but chest-high to the average priest – the drama of communion was acted out. The brass eagle of the lectern, brass candlesticks, flickering candles apart – there were, then, few graven images – the effect was non-conformist.

Under the influence of Principal Halliwell, the services were reasonably "low church" and natural, too. Certainly they were, as far as his sermons were concerned. He preached, as a Parish Priest, homely homilies full of goodness. His fellow Principal, a guest in his Chapel, was a contrast. He began a sermon in the run-up to Christmas with a reference to the fact that, as far as that Christian festival was concerned, "the gastronomical had long superseded the liturgical in the minds of the general populace". We understood him to mean that we enjoyed Christmas dinner more than po-faced Christmas sermons. I'm sure God did, too.

A highlight of one of the services, for the chapel, its congregation and for the clergy, was to be a solo by Stan Jones. A fine tenor – rehearsed, as you already know, often, in the Smoke Hole – he'd been chosen by Prinny White to sing the lovely "Oh! For the Wings of a Dove". We were to "back" him. At rehearsal after rehearsal, we'd thrilled to his singing. T. M. Rhapps, who played the hand-pumped pipe-organ, was more than competent, and Stan and we soared up and down, easily, to the rising, falling, advancing, fading whispers and crescendos of his accompaniment; flying with "La Paloma Blanca".

To this day, T. M. Rhapps – happily hale and hearty – is remembered not only for his superlative playing of the organ but for his "Organ Boots", especially designed, with their soft soles, to get to the soul of the organ as he tendered its pedals with flying feet.

It was the hand-pumping of that organ that cast shadows. Compulsory services were not, themselves, desperately popular. Pumping the organ was. While sermons were on, the organ was silent. Pumpers needn't listen to them. The long handle that they raised and lowered to fill the bellows that blew the pipes was at the left-hand side of the organ as the organist saw it. Behind the organ, there was space for the blowers to rove about, quietly. Above, there was an organ-loft and other recesses of the space over the ante-chapel to explore. Woodbines changed hands, too, we were told. They called them "Holy Smoke".

There was always tension – sometimes coming close to violence – between our choir-master and the pumpers who, in rehearsal, often came scrambling back from more interesting things too late to fill the bellows. Instead of a crashing chord, an asthmatic cough would gasp out. Even more embarrassing sounds, testifying to the broken wind of the instrument, sometimes rapped from it – or should that be "Rhappsed from it"? – in eructation rather than exultation.

Prinny White hated the organ-blowers, hiring and firing them indiscriminately. The pumpers hated him. But somehow, hired or fired, the same few characters always reappeared. They liked the job more than they disliked R. C. White. I'll not name them. Goodness knows what they are now, in their over-ripe old age, but they won't be organ-blowers. Nor are they likely to wish to be reminded of the night of their revenge.

One sacking too many had occurred. The displaced planned vengeance. They had the motive. They had the means. In one of the secret upper places, sacred to organ-blowers, there was a barn-owls' nest. There were young in the nest. The parent birds, used to the noise of the organ and to the coming and going of the pumpers, were not tame but they were tolerant. The father bird was about to star in a Chapel service.

While the new blowers pumped perfectly, filling the organ with music, the old team was up to no good in the organ-loft. They'd been given the sack, and the father owl was in one. As we received signals from the Minor Canon of Winchester Cathedral that it was time for our pièce de resistance, and Stan Jones cleared his throat, unseen, unheard, the sack was carried into position. We stood in our places. The introductory bars of Stan's solo echoed and re-echoed around the church. We waited to take up the chorus. At the very back of the chapel, on a raised dais of several levels, giving us a perfect view of the whole auditorium, we were ready.

"Oh! For the wings, for the wings of a dove!" sang the soloist; his beautiful voice clear; young, a tenor at perfect pitch, he was ringing over the accompaniment.

"Far, far, far, far away would I roam!"

There were the makings of a sacred moment there as the choir prepared to take up the strain of the refrain in four-part harmony. At precisely that moment, and as we did, the sack was emptied out over the organ.

Immediately in front of us, upside down and back to front, in a flurry of feathers, the father Barn Owl tumbled into unsteady flight. Principal White was facing us. His back was to the bird. The congregation faced the altar. Only we and the startled soloist saw the eccentric ornithological entry. Only we saw the owl's Chaplinesque aerobatics – its immediate "grinds and bumps", its loops and swoops, its Immelmann Turns and "falling leaves", as it struggled to right itself. Then, still in our view only, it skimmed close enough to our conductor almost to be skewered by his baton and wheeled away, unsteadily still, but gaining confidence, several feet above the central aisle.

Given the distraction, Stan did magnificently:

"In the wilderness build me, build me a ne-hest", he sang with the panache of a young Pavarotti, even though, by now, the alternative nest-builder was rising into sight of more and more of the congregation.

"And I'll remain there, for ever at rest."

We did our best to live up to him. I doubt that the congregation heard the broken-winded organ-noises that some of us couldn't help making. But the owl was magnificent, too. It was entering into the spirit of the thing and its – now under control – wings took up the beat of the baton.

"Oh ... for the wings ... for the wings ... of a dove", we aspirated, marking as rehearsed, the caesura – that pause, that silence in between sounds – that is as important as the sound itself.

Flaa-ap – pause – flaa-ap – pause – flaa-ap pause, went the flight of the bird. He must have been listening in on our rehearsals and was marking time with the metronome beat of his wings.

The clergy could see the owl now. It was advancing on them. Then the whole congregation watched it as it soared and then dipped again, under the chancel arch. It had, as any convert drawn to redemption, seen the light and was heading for the altar candles.

"There will I build me, build me a ne-est", we sang and, in the spirit of the thing, the lovely white bird alighted and took a closer look at the flickering flame, seeming set "to remain there for ever abreast".

No inquest was held. No arrests were made. No prisoners were taken. The only man in the place who had missed most of the aerial cabaret was our choir conductor. He'd noticed some resistance, some slow entries from us, and worked hard to overcome them. Stan, the trouper, who'd stood up to greater disturbances in the Smoke Hole, had more than satisfied his maestro. The sacked blowers thought honours even, and the candle-courting owl was re-sacked and taken back to his wife and children.

As Tom Sawyer said about the dog and the pinch-bug in church: "Chapel ain't bad when there's a touch of variety to it."

There was more to laugh about for choristers when, on a Harriers trip to compete against the University of Wales, Aberystwyth – where, incidentally, we found ourselves giving running practice to a man who'd beaten Sydney Wooderson in the measured mile somewhere – we travelled up and back by train.

The journey itself was worth more than the pleasures of the race. Our long-ago journey through the heartland of Carmarthenshire to the shores of Cardigan Bay is only possible in part now. The dedication of the officers and members of the Gwili Railway Preservation Society makes that part possible. We can, even now, as they say, "take a nostalgic step into the past along a full-sized, living reminder of a Great Western Railway country branch line." I've promised myself to do that, soon.

For the moment, and with their help in research, I'm able to take you with me and the other Trinity Harriers to the back-end of Carmarthen's third railway station. The first one, opened, as we know, in 1852, was replaced by a second in 1860. We boarded our train to "Aber" from the platform of the one opened in 1902 and still in service. What a litany of place-names lay along the way, easy to set to the poetry of motion of a speeding steam train – if you're a Welsh aboriginal.

Listen to the wheels, the windslip, the bogies, the pistons and the creaking springs as they orchestrate their doggerel.

> Bronwydd Arms, Cwmdwyfran, Penybont:
> Such sounds as a rhymer would want
> To set to the speed of the train
> Meand'ring the Gwili, where rain,
> Now settling softer than dew,
> Is gentling the winter – and you
> In the lilt and the lust of your youth …
> Let's end there, just short of the truth.

But, liquid as the turning and twisting river, the syllables of Llwyfan Cerrig, Conwil, Llanpumsaint, slip off the native tongue of a Dafydd Oliver. The once-prosaic New Quay Road – put back into poetry as Bryn Teifi, in that other wartime year, 1916: Maesycrugiau, Llanybyther, Pencarreg Halt, Lampeter, and the Bettws (that became an alien-sounding Derry Ormond, as early as 1874) go by as our train runs on – the syllables in Llangybi, Olmarch (where it Halts!), Pont Llanio, Tregaron, Alltddu, Strata Florida – Well, Welsh is Latin-based! – and the trailing veils of mist, tumbling waters and dripping trees of Caradoc Falls tell us that Trawscoed, Felin Dyffryn, Llanilar and Llanrhystyd Road are signalling us into Aberystwyth. There is the mystique, what's more, of taking on "Uni Students". Training college "types" and "varsity" fellows were further apart then than the ends of a railway journey.

One of our runners was both a chorister and some sort of functionary of the College Chapel. Aberystwyth, as a university town, had a superior retail book facility. Our friend was asked to make a purchase on behalf of the chapel of a gross of hymn-books. He'd carried an extra canvas knap-sack to stow them in and, when we boarded the train for our return journey, he hung the bag of books from the coat-hook on the overhead rack.

On the bends and turns of the track, where it ran through steep and wooded cuttings, that bag became a nuisance, yo-yoing to and fro and, occasionally, bumping a head or two! We were an excited group. One of us became over-excited.

"What's this damn thing doing?" he yelled. "Nobody needs this?"

And he picked it off the hook and pretended to hurl it through the open window. He intended the bag of books to go out to the full length of the shoulder-strap and to come back in again. He'd failed to notice the cutting's steep sides or the speed at which the train was running up to and passing the railside telephone posts with their steel hawser supports.

The bag went out to the length of the strap alright but it never came back. Indeed, it was lucky that the man who threw it didn't follow it, either from the drag of its exit – an enormous pull on his hands before he let go of it – or from the rage of the lad whose responsibility the books were. Both of them, in a moment, were ashen pale: the one with anger, the other from sheer fright. They rushed to the carriage window in time to see the bag still wrapping itself round and around the hawser, ten feet from the ground. Apparently, it was still there when the rail "gangers" recovered it on the following Monday. Eventually, the hymn-books reached their intended destination, and so did we. Our sympathy for the two Harriers involved had been total. The tears were still in our eyes as we ran, backwards, into Carmarthen Station. Hysterics do that to you.

There came a time when the demands of the choir conflicted with real life. Always a sufferer from tonsilitis and inclined to lose my voice – especially on the touch-line at rugby matches – I went to see Principal White. Taking a minder with me and speaking as throatily as I could, I explained my problems and said that, regretfully, I should resign.

He was very understanding. In fact, he was much more understanding than I'd expected him to be.

"I understand your regret, Parry", he said. "I understand your not wanting to sing with a sore throat and such. So what can we do about it?" I failed to notice the glint behind the glass of his gold-framed spectacles.

He paused for a moment before delivering the most unhelpful, helpful solution to my problems.

"I've been intending to appoint a Choir Secretary: someone who would see to the chores such as making certain that all the chaps are up and about in good time for early communion and that: to keep a general sort of eye on things. Why don't I appoint you? That way, you can still be a part of the choir without having to sing in it." It was a rhetorical question, of course. My acceptance of the honour was implied.

From then on, I was a dogsbody. I'd accentuated the disadvantages of choir membership – having to get up even earlier on Sundays and Saints' days. My friends resented my having to get them to the church on time. What's more, set to stand among them while, officially, not singing with them, I couldn't throw back my head and belt into my favourite hymns – the greatest advantage of choir membership – because that would mean that Prinny White had won. Whatever else he might or might not have been, one thing was certain. He was Machiavelli set to music and knew what a ruler must do to retain power in his tiny state.

There is one positive, though, to be entered in the man's favour. It was the custom in Trinity, then, to hold an Eisteddfod on or around St. David's Day. I entered for the Public Speaking competition. Not a profound affair, it was really an "impromptu" speaking contest. Held in the Broadcast Hall, it was adjudicated by the Rev. R. C. White. We were invited to draw our subject from a box of topics. I put in my hand and drew out: "THAT NEIGHBOUR, ENGLAND".

If I were Tony Benn, I would present you, now, with the entire text of that fifty-year-old speech. I would have gone straight to my desk after uttering it and captured it for posterity. Few of us have so well-developed a sense of history-in-the-making as the veteran Member for Chesterfield.

History, however, made my speech for me. I began by regretting that I was not an historian, cravenly apologised for being a geographer, and confessed that I didn't know whether it was Napoleon or Josephine who looked on England as a neighbour. There was something about "Little England Beyond Wales", and about how hard it is to love one's neighbours, especially when they're English. Prinny White found it amusing. He gave me first prize. My friends found that amusing!

CHAPTER EIGHT

The Strike

You might remember that, early on in this memoir, I wrote of Trinity College being "run as though its students were still at school". "Its General Prefect", I added, "was the Head Boy. The Students' Council was an extension of the College establishment." My first claim was right. In respect of the other two, in 1943-'44, I was totally wrong.

I was right again, though, when I said: "The democracy that some of those arriving with us had been fighting to preserve hadn't even reached Trinity." There were to be interesting times ahead in the cloistered corridors of College power but no conflict, "yet".

You'll recall the disparity between white table-linen and our rainbowed cloths. You know of our half-biscuit tins. I've pointed out the age-ranges among students and the administration's failure to recognise a growing problem. "Those times, they were a'changing so swiftly that the system was about to be shaken to its foundation." Conflict was near.

H. L. Harby's famous "Wing" no longer serves as it once did. "Calfaria is a super-market, now." Reduced from accommodation to administration – gutted, with no second door on the right on which to hang a plaque announcing "Gordon Parry slept here" – its inter-war austerity no longer suitable to the student sophisticates of the second half of the twentieth century, who even knew what a bidet was for before going on their school's skiing holiday in Cortina d'Ampesso. It has been outclassed and replaced by towering halls of residence, hostels with "en-suite" facilities. "One man, one room" ceased to operate soon after our days in the Wing. Subsequent students were two to a room. There must have been some agony for the College management in that decision, and some serious strains on tolerance between the two forced to share a room designed for one. Our intake was more fortunate even than our junior year.

Principal Clive Jones-Davies, today, has to house more than 600 resident students on campus out of his total college population of 1,600. Principal Tom Halliwell was host to a total, all male, all in residence, roll of 126 in 1943; a register that only expanded to 130 through 1944 to 1945.

Even then, in our second year, the Wing couldn't give single rooms to them all. The College had to fall back on using dormitory accommodation that it had expected to vacate for ever. To say that it had been left dormant since the Wing had been built was more than a pun. It was to be an extension of the problems that came to a head over general house-keeping at Trinity and the open and dramatic parting of the ways between the administration and the Students' Council during early 1944. The Council grew up. It stopped being puppet of, and party to, the Establishment. Trinity, at the same moment, stopped being a Sixth Form College. It grew up, too.

If I ever knew, I no longer do, what individual event triggered the break. Certainly, there had been a build-up of tension. We all knew about that. There had been growing dissatisfaction about academic and domestic arrangements.

The staff, in numbers and speciality, had been overstretched. Lecture-rooms were overcrowded. Individual lecturers were forced beyond their own competencies, taking on areas of study that were unfamiliar to them. The excellent Dai Griff (in hygiene and health education) wasn't far into horticulture and recommended clothing "made of linen from the ... from the ... from the linen plant". It wasn't a serious uncertainty but those of us from Pembrokeshire who'd spent some time on day-release at Bierspool Farm, pulling flax for the war effort, were able later to tease him. Older staff-men had more serious difficulty of adjustment, chief among them in recognising that they were teaching a number of maturer men.

The real focus of discontent was domestic, and we were not the only residents in that under-serviced Victorian building. There were furry friends as well.

The reopened dormitories were, as I've indicated, above the dining-hall and kitchens. They hadn't been unoccupied when they were unoccupied. It was discovered, dramatically, that the rodent population was high and, it seems, resentful of being disturbed by two-legged creatures. I encountered Roland the Rat myself, one night, while caring for the sick.

One of my charges, in my post as runner to the doctor, was running ahead of my brief. On "aspirin and rest", his temperature had soared. There was no response to my knocking on Captain Ithel Thomas's door. I set off to tell the Principal.

Uncertain of finding unlocked interior doors or lights on after "Lights Out", I made my way around the outside walls of the then Library building, down past the eastern wall of the Chapel and round on to the front lawns of the main entrance, under its twin sentinels – the "Monkey Puzzle" Chile Pines – and approached the door of the Principal's residence.

It had been dark all the way but, from where I was, I could see far away down to the Pembrokeshire road home. Only the occasional spilling of light marked it for me. There was traffic there, of course, but all motor vehicles went masked along the highway at night. The headlamps wore black metal visors with movable shutters that ensured that the car, lorry or motor-bike moved in its own ambience of light that ended well within its braking distance. Sidelights were bound with masking tape pierced by a small hole, the size of a silver three-penny bit. Interior lights were forbidden. "Put that light out!" was a cry not confined to the corridors of the Wing. German bombing crews, their planes throbbing through the upper dark, only needed an incautious naked light to find targets.

Naturally enough, we'd become more conscious of the night sky in the absence of ground lights. From Principal Halliwell's doorstep, I was able to see a myriad stars winking – advancing, receding – about the Milky Way. I even knew the names of many of them. My Air Training Corps service – which I had hoped to have converted into membership of the University Air Squadron, Carmarthen College Flight – had taught me them. They were – I'd checked them – in their proper places, as I yanked the handle of the Principal's door-bell. It rang loudly. In a moment or two, the door opened and the man himself stepped out, closing the door behind him to preserve the "black-out".

"It's Parry, Sir", I said. "I'm on sick duty. There's a man very unwell, Sir."

"Parry, my boy", said Mr. Halliwell, who might or might not have known me then – in so small a college population, he probably did. "Do step inside a moment. I must come with you to see him. I'll just get a torch."

I stepped inside – just – as he closed the door and made off down the corridor-cum-conservatory. I'd hardly time to adjust to the inside light when the Principal was back.

"Come this way, Parry", he said. "There's no need for us to go outside. We'll go through the Dining Hall."

There was, off a passage-way, a heavy connecting door. I was abreast of the Principal as, opening the door, he clicked the light switches that lit the Hall. "Gracious me!" he exclaimed, clicking them off and immediately clicking them on and off again. I had seen what he had seen; a rat in the middle of a dining-table, gathering scraps from a table-cloth. Since experts say that, if you see one rat, there are ten more within twenty yards of it, we must have sent a plague of them scuttling for cover. As the lights came on again, this time to a ratless table, we made our way down the length of the place to the Cloisters door. Neither of us mentioned what we had seen.

My disturbing the Principal was justified. Dr. Humphreys was 'phoned. She came and examined the lad. The student was sent to hospital with a suspected swollen appendix, after she'd checked him out. His early influenza had disguised more serious symptoms.

There was to be a much more dramatic encounter with a rat when my contemporary Brian Beresford, promoted in charge of a re-opened dormitory, found one in bed with him. Brian objected strenuously to sharing, and was bitten seriously on the nose. He was hospitalised, too, but I wasn't involved with his case!

As was every other student, I was involved in THE STRIKE. Just as an Army "marches on its stomach", our stomachs took us into revolt.

The food seemed to be going from bad to worse. Some of the dishes were incredible and inedible. Even then, there were some that were edible, and we came close to fighting over these. A good trencherman myself, brought up to eat at the next meal anything that I had refused at the last, and having an older brother only too anxious to devour what I was slow to enjoy, I could manage most things. It was a bonus to some of us when tenderer souls – the only sons of indulgent parents – couldn't. Very little went back from our table, and the fight that nearly was, was called when evident unfairness in distribution saw a larger than lion's share go to a senior who was actually a Pembrokeshire man from North of the Landsker.

I wasn't a Nonconformist and a nephew of Ianto Bolshie for nothing. I questioned that student's morality, his greed and his parentage. He challenged me to fight him, that afternoon, behind the gym.

For the third time in my life, I was called out. At Neyland Board School, because he'd taken my ball, I'd been rushed into a ring, drawn in the gravel, to fight "Guzzer" Rees. By then, I was ready to give him the ball, but the die was cast. As we circled one another, both willing to go home if they'd let us, a bigger boy, crying "Get on with it!", pushed me violently in the back. Poor Guzzer caught the brunt of it. Flailing for balance, I hit him high on the nose. I hadn't seen his nose; hadn't been looking for it; was trying to find my own feet, but my reputation was made as the blood spurted. His eyes were so black next morning that in our caring school we both had the cane for fighting. I never had to fight again at primary level and had an inconclusive "You step over that line, then, boy, and see what will happen!" sort of pushing and shoving bout with a lanky lad called John Grey in secondary school.

But this fight over food thing at Trinity was serious. I was to strike a blow for the underprivileged by taking on a chap who looked as big as I was and was – at that table, anyway – better fed. It was almost serious enough to put me off my food. Fortunately, it didn't. Regretting that I now had to put my body where my mouth had been, I went, with my seconds, to the duelling ground. We stood around until long after "Zero Hour". The enemy didn't turn up. I was glad that I had. I moved further up the table next day, and ate as much as he did. He was sheepish but silent over his lamb and mint sauce and his greasy gravy.

The meal that was the most memorable and could – even on its own – have precipitated revolt was the rabbit hot-pot. Growing up in Pembrokeshire, son of a man with farming in his blood and a mother who could cook like an angel, I'd eaten the lean, luscious, sweet meat of the rabbit in a dozen different styles. Mother Owen's treatment of the coney had to be seen to be believed!

Delivered to our table, by a student on kitchen duty, in an enamel Army-surplus pan that had been battered black in patches, probably at Mons, a whole buck-rabbit floated in thin gravy. As the pan was set down, the parboiled corpse floated to the surface. It looked as if it had been plucked and feathered rather than skinned. I swear that it still had its furry feet on, but others will contest that.

It did "look", though. It looked at us, balefully. Its head had not been detached, and its hard-boiled eyes were still in place. "There!" said our colleague, the conscripted skivvy. "What d'you make of that, then? That ought to see you through the day!" Some said that the thing from the deep winked an eye at that.

These things actually occurred. Allow for hyperbole in the recounting. Discount something for the fifty years' distance between events and reportage. But, believe me, they occurred.

Cecil Parry maintains to this day that the only reason why the ageing College horse, that hauled the plough for the Rural Scientists, was paraded past the Dining Hall windows every evening was to reassure us that we hadn't eaten it. Not yet!

It would be impossible now to date these occurrences exactly between September, 1943 and July, 1945. Nor does anyone who was involved know now which of them happened first and which last, or the order of their happening in between.

Together, and with many other irritant and corrosive distractions from general harmony, they brought anger and frustration with them to the representatives of the students and a refusal to recognise the dangers of that to the administration. The inevitable happened. The sides stopped communicating. Why speak when no-one was listening?

There was a difference in this deadlock, though. The Establishment wasn't dealing with boys any more. It was dealing with men, who, having faced up to Nazis, weren't going to surrender the pass to the Dean of St. Davids. There was also the fact that Richard Fry was mature by nature.

An unsavoury event, I believe, around the end of our first term, with Christmas in the offing, had left a bad smell and a bitter taste. It involved a rumbustious, rugby-playing friend of most of us, whose name I know well but won't use. He is alive and fit, having enjoyed at least four careers, as an Army officer, in war, a Royal Air Force officer, in peace, as administrator of a national body, and, though it can't have been for long, as a teacher. Let's call him A. N. Other.

You need to know about the legend of the "Mad Monk of Trinity". A wholly fictitious character, out of the minds of a group of practical jokers, his "ghost" began to appear – or was said to appear – around the place. This shadowy figure, in hood and habit, appeared and disappeared against the moonlight within the grounds. Once, it was glimpsed for a split-second in silhouette by many, many people leaving a concert in the Broadcast Hall.

The Monk made for good conversation. There were even those who believed the legend. And it grew. It must have been a starlit Saturday evening when A. N. Other took that legend and the Mad Monk in hand.

We've said nothing, yet, though we will, in time, of the courting of the girls and the serious growing-up that was going on extramurally. Some lads were lucky enough to have met nurses from St. David's Hospital, the other Victorian building, higher up the hill, behind Trinity. Wednesday and Saturday matinées were good for such meetings. So was the road to and from the town.

The hospital was known, in those days, as "The Asylum" and catered for the mentally disturbed. Its patients were nursed by some of the loveliest girls in West Wales. Their ages ranged. Some, the probationers, were younger than we were. Others were older. It was the fantasy of many of the College's more repressed youths to be adopted by a 30-year-old Ward Sister and to become her "kept man". One of my friends confessed to me that he'd been fantasising about nurses ever since he'd had his tonsils out. Short of becoming a gigolo, he would happily settle down, he said, as the kept man of a Ward Sister. Unfortunately, he was not a man, and the job-specification "Toy Boy" hadn't then been written.

Whether A. N. Other had a permanent attachment or not, he was walking home from town with several other couples on a Saturday evening when the puppeteers behind the legend had decided to make the Mad Monk walk again. A. N. Other and the others were approaching the college gates at somewhere about the point where the car-park opens out today (then it was a marshy field with a high hedge between it and the road) when the Monk moved. Several large ash-trees grew out of the hedge to a height of some thirty feet and more. Deep in the shadow that they threw, the spectral figure of the Mad Monk rose in the road. It seemed nine feet tall, and moaning, groaning sounds came from that deeper darkness.

The nurses screamed and ran. Their escorts – only because they were anxious not to lose them, of course – ran after them.

Whoever heard of a gigolo who wasn't ready to run with his keeper? Not A. N. Other: he didn't even stand fast. As all the others, other than Other, ran away, old "A.N.", as we shall now call him, ran at the dancing spirit.

"Come here, you bugger!" he shouted. "I'll give you Monk, you swine!" and, in the finest traditions of the rugby field that he graced, regularly, he launched himself into a flying tackle.

In the field above, behind an ash-tree, the Mad Monk's operators were taken by surprise. They had, earlier, fixed a clothes-line pulley high in the tree. The line that they held in hand passed up and through the pulley and down to a coat-hanger that had been sewn into a Noel Coward-style, stagey, velvet, dressing-gown with a high hood. As our "A.N." struck the puppet-Monk, the line, snatched from their hands, whirred through the pulley and fell to the road. Kneeling on the handsome dressing-gown, A. N. Other heard the whirring and was up in a flash after a new target. Scrambling up the hedge, yelling through the blackthorn, he was only in time to catch a glimpse of hurtling shadows and to hear the pounding of feet as he ripped his trousers on barbed wire.

Later, but not too late for Compline, for which we were all gathering, "A.N." walked into the urinals off the Cloisters. The story had run before him. At the last stop before Chapel, some in the stalls, some out of them, the lads demanded the tale from his own mouth. Flushed from his heroism, proud of his triumph, "Well boys! I got a bloody good dressin'-gown out of it", he launched into his rococo account, florid, furious, fulminating. His language was highly ornamented, but this was an excited young man in full throat to an audience of admiring young males who were egging him on.

Unfortunately for all of them, and most unfortunately for A. N. Other, a lavatory door behind the group opened and Principal Halliwell stood there, framed in the doorway, as several sound, echo and sense words out of the origins of the language brought our hero's tirade to an end. The Principal, who had heard the whole thing, was enraged. Redder than red, his face quivered, his lips trembled, and he seemed close to tears. None came. Nor did any sound break. Students tried to pretend that they weren't there. Then, the Rev. Mr. Halliwell – truly shaken in his soul, I believe – swung angrily away, having said nothing, and the group was left pole-axed. In minutes, there came a message instructing A. N. Other to report to the Principal's office.

The Compline service was quieter than usual. Given what we already know of the general conducting of the religious life of Trinity College during the 'forties, the service in itself was an unexpected Anglican hangover from the Church of Rome. The "completed hour" – the last of the seven canonical hours of the divine office – with its Saturday evening observance, was an act of discipline imposed, regardless of creed or denomination, on all students then.

We'd been – those who knew about the Mad Monk, the outraged Principal and the discomfitted hero – shocked going into Compline. We were more shocked coming out. This had been the completing hour for A. N. Other. Some had thought that he might be rusticated for his use of "bad language". He had, in fact, been "sent down". Rustication, as a punishment, meant a cooling-off period "in the country". Being sent down was terminal.

Either then or very shortly thereafter, a notice appeared on the bulletin board, signed by the Principal. It confirmed that the sentence of college death was effective, there and then. It carried an even crueller sting in its tail. Since A. N. Other's place in College had been withdrawn from him, "the appropriate authority" had been informed, and the man would become "subject to call-up for military service" immediately. That news, of course, was not for A. N. Other – he'd gone. It was a warning to all of us that we were students "on borrowed time": be careful or be soldiers.

As I've said, after 50 years I'm not certain in which order these unsettling things occurred. Nor do I know what combination of aggravations and frustrations had led the Principal to such instant and such Draconian punishment. Thomas Halliwell had been in the Navy himself, he told us later, and had still been shocked by the "language" that he'd overheard, by accident, in the Bogs. Today, he'd hear little girls using such words in the street, but he surely knew that – on their own with fellows and out of bravado – men used such words to dramatise their masculinity.

Mind you, there were those who had fallen foul of A. N. Other's robust rowdiness who thought the punishment matched the crime: especially those who'd been Cherry-Blossomed!

Years later, when I was in bed in Glangwili Hospital, fighting my way back to health from that accident that broke my bones, rearranged my features and my legs, collapsed my lung and stove in my ribs, my father, coming to visit me, was himself in a motor accident at Dryslwyn and was brought in to Ceri Ward, where he died, only yards from me. Principal Halliwell, caring, kind and comforting, came to visit me and made certain, over a long period of recuperation, that I wanted for nothing.

As for A. N. Other, he proved that there's never an ill-wind that doesn't blow some good. He was a commissioned officer in the Army before anyone of us was a certificated teacher. He took a taste for the Services but, when he was "demobbed" after the war ended, he returned to college, completed his qualification, and spent time in teaching before re-mustering into commissioned rank in the Royal Air Force, since when he has served Wales – especially the youth of Wales – with unbroken distinction.

In the post-war years, then, specific apologies must have been offered and amends made to the satisfaction of both men but, in general terms, the bigger break caused the most public disquiet.

There came a day when the General Prefect and the Students' Council called us out on strike.

We attended a "mass" meeting, in traditional protest style. We were told of deadlock in discussions, and a total failure to secure any concessions improving the domestic housekeeping and feeding in the College. The presence of the rodents was cited. We knew that we had a reasonable set of grievances. But the ultimate grievance was that grown men – some, very mature and travelled men – were being expected to behave like schoolboys and do what they were told. Men who had served their country already couldn't be threatened with their "call-up". The choice of the protest march and its destination to focus attention on our discontent was brilliant.

Our ultimate complaint being housekeeping, in general, and the standards of cuisine, in particular, we were to gather in the College drive before noon and to march from there, together, into and across town, to the British Restaurant.

"Where and what is the British Restaurant?" you might ask. The answer to the first question is: it was in a large stone building, roughly opposite to the shopping complex on John Street in the area of the main car-park there. The answer to the second question is: the British Restaurant was created during the war to make available good food at cost price to war workers, civilians, service personnel and to anyone who had need of it. Supplementary to the rations – I'm not sure, now, whether we needed to show our Ration Books, but I don't think so – the meals were excellent. Every reasonably sized town had one. They continued to open for business certainly into the late 1940s. As a teacher, in town on a Saturday, I used to eat at the excellent British Restaurant in Haverfordwest.

Before we began the march, we were advised to behave responsibly. Our only demonstration was to be the march itself, and our very public meal in town. Both Dai Griff and H. L. Harby and – I seem to remember – Llew Llewellyn had quiet words with some of us. They, too, advised good behaviour, indicated support for the object of the campaign, and gave the impression that our arguments were close to acceptance.

Before setting out, we were issued with Restaurant tokens. The full meal, of three courses and a cup of tea, cost less than my mother paid Joe Davies for a sack of coal. I think that the Students' Council bought the tokens and met their cost. A two-shilling piece – the silver florin from my mother's leather purse – was one-tenth of the old £1 note. The appropriate coin in decimals would be 10p.

We behaved impeccably, waited in line to enter the Restaurant, which had obviously known of our coming, were called by our seniors and seated as space became available, ate a magnificent meal, and then formed up again and marched back to Trinity.

The Dean of St. Davids had moved in. Crisis meetings were convened. It was clear that we were going to eat out again unless eating-in became a far better option than it had been. Whether we did so more than once, I can't confirm, now. I think not.

We'd won, though. The quiet nature of the strike and the interest that it caused, together with the "solidarity" of the students and the quality of their leadership, ensured that we had won as soon as we crossed the threshold of the campus. The gown had gone to town and won itself a victory.

Among the concessions were additions to the domestic staff, a wholesale spring-cleaning of college buildings, and the calling in of the rat-catchers. Dozens and dozens of rodents were caught and killed, their nests destroyed, their accesses closed. The infamous kitchen-duty became voluntary and then, of course, we competed to do it. Tom Sawyer could have told them that.

There were additions – in time – to the academic staff, and it seemed that Dean Parry was rather less often around. Perhaps the strike had really brought students and staff to the same priorities, and Principal Halliwell was a happier man after that. I was having the time of my life.

Jim Davies wasn't. His walk back to Boncath had come to a halt. For five months and more, he'd been holed up in a loft – a vegetable store – in the roof of a friendly farm-house in Garijp, in Holland. Each morning, he ate a simple "but adequate" breakfast. In the afternoon, he took a main meal of "hot potatoes, cabbage, and sometimes a little meat". For ever afterwards, he was to associate Sunday "with the weekly boiled egg". The brave Dutch family in whose roof-space he lived during those months were risking everything – including their own lives – to keep him hidden.

There were worse billets than those offered at Trinity College, Carmarthen, for the late-teenagers of Europe in 1943 to 1945! We were aware of that, though we had no means of knowing that our future friend and colleague had to sit-out "124 long days and nights" of waiting, as British troops fought their way towards him. Nor that, by the time they reached there, he would be gone.

CHAPTER NINE

The Girls

Our food had improved remarkably. So had the kitchen staff. Two girls appeared there: the one, Irish and pretty, the other, Welsh and friendly. We talked about girls all the time and, in free time, roaming in packs, hunted for "talent".

We went on "the bunny run". The term seems to have originated in Tredegar, where a specific route up and down the street culminated, on Saturdays and Sundays, under the ornate town clock. Successful "bunny hunters" then lolloped off, white-tailed and bouncy, with their bright-eyed does, for a more personal walk around Tredegar Park. Chapel-taught, I might have avoided a Park that had a sentence from Dante's "Inferno" worked into its wrought-iron gates. "ABANDON HOPE ALL YE WHO ENTER HERE", it said. I wonder why?

At Neyland, our hopes of friendship took us "round the Prom". There was a promenade, specifically built for promenading in 1911, that ran along the beach from Picton Road to a bridge over the Pulks. In 1937 and 1938, my sisters, Hilda and Mary, with their friends, loved to walk "round the Prom", evocatively dressed in their flowing, floral "Beach Pyjamas", closely followed by the lads of their fancy. Both the fashion and the tradition died with the war.

In Carmarthen, such things were less structured for us. There was a walk along the river bank, down below the Ivy Bush Hotel. I remember sitting on a bench there with a lovely girl who had taken me by the hand in the Lyric. I'd met her inside – not by arrangement, I hasten to add – by accident. It was a late October, early November, evening, one of those rare ones that begin in an Indian Summer afternoon.

Leaving Trinity soon after our Harriers' running was over – fired by the deep-heat of that and the subsequent shower – I'd dressed lightly, for the sun. That had been a mistake. I was underdressed for sun-down, and the sun was down before my new-found friend and I left the Lyric. Our first call was for tea and toast at the café opposite. The lass was a joy to be with, particularly there, where envious friends were gathered. What's more, she was identified with one of our friends who wasn't there. His travel arrangements had gone wrong. An away game for the College had played extra time. Stranded somewhere, "up the line", his loss had become my gain. There was, in a closed society, status in that.

What's more, I had enough of my five-shilling Postal Order left to pay for her tea and toast. There was status in that, too, as I stepped to the till flourishing a florin – the only coin I had – as though there were plenty more where that lonely piece of silver came from. In terms of loss and gain, the tea-shop was up; Tabernacle Chapel would be down when, at morning service, the collection-plate came round.

Outside, the evening air was chilling. There wasn't a cloud in the sky to hold down any of the heat of the afternoon. I wished that I had my scarf, or my tie even, and buttoned my shirt with my left hand, holding tightly to my friendly friend with the right.

"Let's go down by the river", she said.

Still a relative stranger in town, I scarcely knew where that was. The meanders of the Tywi left me confused. I knew where the bridge was but hadn't caught up with the ins and outs and round-abouts of the river yet. My lady had walked its banks before. I was happy to go where she led, although I might have hoped for a warmer destination: a brief encounter in the Railway Station's Waiting Room, perhaps. There was a fire there most evenings.

By this time, I was almost into hypothermia. The only warm bits of me were down my right side, where she was snuggled against me. Not overdressed herself, she still generated comfort. It was giving a new dimension to "hot-stuff". The rest of me was slowly becoming frozen-paralysed.

As I fervently hoped for a wind-break somewhere, a cwtch in a corner out of the draught, we came to a knoll above the Tywi. A provident Borough Council, thinking warm, summer afternoons, had set a seat at the top of it. That cold, clear evening, there was a full moon low in the West Wales sky but, naturally, there was no sun.

The view was spectacular. You know how the Tywi wanders? That night, it meandered, silver in the moonlight, through a succession of shades and shadows that were almost colours in themselves. In the black-out, there were no ground-lights to distract the eye and limit the perception. There was the deep-purple black of the sky. There were the stars. There was the moon. There was the girl. "G-gi-me the moonlight. G-gi-me the girl, an' leave the rest to me".

The setting was perfect. It was the temperature that was the trouble. How do Eskimos manage? But then, I'd have exchanged that exposed bench for a snugly igloo, on the spot.

It wasn't very gallant of me to sit eastward of that lovely girl. The night wind off the river had come over the estuary from the south-west. The mercury moon had come up with it, cold and comfortless but bringing beauty out of the darkness, quick-silvering the Tywi, highlighting the valley and the dumpling hills as far as the Bishop's Palace at Abergwili, silhouetting and shadowing the taller trees and the eaves of the nearer buildings, while all down my left side I was into a minor stroke.

I'd been about to tell my new-found love the names of the stars. There they were, hanging up there, millions of light-years and hyper-cold space-nights away, waiting to be recognised. I hadn't been out with a girl yet who hadn't been impressed when I pointed to and named Castor and Pollux, Dubhe and Bennetnash, Polearis, the Plough and the Great Bear.

D'you know, I couldn't raise my left arm above my shoulder? There is such a thing as "a frozen shoulder". I was left with one after that car crash, and mighty painful it was. My park-bench paralysis was not that, but my shoulder was frozen stiff. My hand shook as I tried to point the path along the blade of the Plough to the North Star. My lips were taut across my teeth, and the tightening and refrigeration of other nerves, muscles and mechanisms had raised my tenor voice to mezzo-soprano.

"That", I tried to point out and to say, "is Polearis." I sounded like my mother singing "Beulah Land", as she often did, off-key, as she often was.

The whole thing about pointing out the stars was the way in which a girl's face tilted up as you guided her eyes to the heavens. Weak though my effort was, it was working now. Hers was a beautiful face, too. Her golden daylight hair, darkened by night, was lit from behind by the moon, a silver lining to a passing autumn cloud – and her eyes caught the moonlight as she looked through stars at the stars. That woman-child was alive, breathing high in her nostrils, her full lips smiling up at me, her perfect teeth, traced by the tip of her tongue, whiter than white in the shadows, and she was warm with it!

The moment had come. I lowered my lips to hers, forgetting that mine were frozen in my face, and that my nose was an icicle as cold as that of a healthy Husky dog. Talk about romancing the stone! Shivering, chilled to the marrow, not only had my sense of feeling atrophied but my judgement of distance was gone. We were closer than I'd thought. With no lips between them to cushion the clash, our teeth rattled together, ringing like the cups dancing in their saucers as Nellie Roach had clumped around Mrs. Samuel Davies's tea-table. The shock was painful but nothing like the pain to come.

As I'd leaned across, shifting the weight from my right foot to my left – with my left leg, extended behind me, taking a sudden strain from the ball of the foot to the head of the femur – every muscle in it, involuntarily and simultaneously, knotted into cramp.

My hamstring twanged like a long-bow; my calf-muscles caffled like binder twine; and, in the bottom of my buttock, where the left cheek of my behind had been stretched across the fishmonger's slab of the seat, something important exploded. So did I. Added together, it was trauma. Like Dai Griff hurtling off the trampoline, I shot up in the air, taking my partner totally by surprise. Our attempt at a kiss had been fumbled. There had been no fire in it: no warmth. She clearly hadn't expected my reaction to it to be so energetic. My reflex bound had taken me up and on to her. For a moment, I straddled her. My right knee was on her side of the bench and my left was leaping about over her right thigh. My right arm was pinned under her and my left clutching at her lean and lissom body for support. My left foot, meanwhile, heel to toe, was arched the wrong way, cranked up against my backside, and the pain would have made a spartan cry out!

I don't know what that girl was thinking then. "True Romance" and the "News of the World" were full of stories of passionate men losing control, and the sons of the clergy often figured in them. If she was still optimistic of our get-together in the moonlight, she might have expected me – even with all that leaping about – to "spare a sweet word of love" or, mistaking my agony for ecstasy, to hear me growl out my devotion like the ever-angry, ever-scowling James Mason in the arms of Margaret Lockwood. "Kiss me like they do in the Pictures" belonged to a generation, not just to Dylan Thomas.

Life, particularly at seventeen, as she was, is so full of unfulfilled expectation. With my face a hair's breadth from hers, I howled "C-RAMP-UH!" and fell off her, backwards, on to the grass. A Harrier, I knew what I had to do. Kicking off my shoe, kicking out my foot, stretching out my lower leg – despite the screaming pain of it – pressing my knee down flat on the ground, pulling my toes back, I came through the worst of it. There was no chill now. I was sweating from the shock of the seizure and the white-heat of re-entry.

For a moment, I lay on my back on the grass, my groaning done. Then, that lovely girl came tumbling after me. She was laughing with all her lungs.

"Cu-RAMP-Uh!" she shouted. "Cu-RAMP-Uh!" and we both rolled about on the dewy grass, all arms and legs and tender fun. It was so very, very funny, now, and there was no serious growing-up to be done that night.

Well! We kissed – several times – just as they did in the pictures then, with no-one eating any one else's face, until, with those thawed lips close to my still frost-bitten ear, she whispered softly: "D'you fancy some chips in a bag? I've got money because you paid for tea."

Incredibly, we never went out together again, and there came a moment when her belated boy-friend stopped me in the North Hall.

"Hey! Sam!" he said. "I want to thank you for looking after my girl-friend. She said you were very nice to her; bought her tea and toast. She asked me to give you her love, and hopes your leg's better. What happened to your leg, Sam?"

"Just a little bit of cramp", I said. "You know, Harrying, an' that."

I'd missed out on true romance but, now, I'd made a new college mate. You notice that I've named neither of them. Mates didn't do that then, and I won't do it now. They are probably somebody's great grandparents, if they're still alive and together. If she is, then she should know that – in my 70th year – I think of her kindly and, if her husband and my wife would allow it, I'd love to limp with her along the river bank again – as long as it was a summer afternoon, and the sun was shining on that grassy knoll. "G-gi-me the sunlight, g-gi-me the girl and leave the rest to me!" Or, as that Trinity student cried, fifty years ago and more: "Cu-RAMP-Uh!"

You will have gathered that Cecil Parry – the schoolmate who'd referred me to my clerical referee was, as my close Wing neighbour and colleague in Trinity, a growing influence on me. Bright, with an aptitude for study that had marked him as a scholar in Portsmouth and in Pembroke Dock, he was enjoying the college life as much as I was, if, perhaps, a little more sedately.

"He's a wise young owl is Cecil", my mother said of him once. He wore glasses in dark frames that were heavier than most. His studious appearance was enhanced by them. "You could do worse than listen to Cecil."

I did listen to him quite a bit. He had little option but to listen to me, too, and I reported to him my Saturday evening adventures at the riverside. He said little at the time but filed it in his good brain for future reference. The future came sooner than you might have thought.

One day, in Woolworths, I discovered – appropriately, behind the sweet counter – as beautiful a girl as I'd ever seen. She was of an age with me, lithe, elegant, and blessed with those green-to-amber eyes that complement and compliment darkly auburn hair. Her complexion shaded auburn and amber into olive skin and, when she smiled, as she did at me, the Song of Solomon sang in my head where I stood beside the rationed Liquorice All-Sorts. It wouldn't have taken much for me to say: "Thy teeth are like a flock of sheep that are even shorn, which came up from the washing; where of every one bear twins, and none is barren among them. Thy lips are like a thread of scarlet, and thy speech is comely."

It wouldn't have taken much. 'Thees" and Thous" were still in use in the Pembrokeshire of my childhood. The Authorised Version rang through our chapel and I had a great deal of it in my head. What I really said was: "Do you come here often?"

She shamed me by accepting my silliness as serious. "Yes, every day of the week", she said, "an' I've seen you here before, too."

"Never!" said I, still fighting for a line. "You can't have seen me before, without my seeing you. I couldn't possibly have missed you."

"Perhaps you weren't looking for me, Love", she teased.

"I'm looking now, though", I said, earnestly.

"You spend a lot of time in here, looking at the girls, don't you, Love?" she asked. Every time she said "Love", I lost more ground. This beautiful, direct and most unusual girl already had me in thrall. You don't expect the Queen of Sheba to live in Pontyates and to sell sweets in Woolworths in Carmarthen. Read the 4th chapter of Solomon's "Song of Love" to remind yourself of what I mean, and what that moment meant to adolescent me.

"Can I wait for you, then, and stop looking for anyone else, Love?" I asked, emphasising the "love". "Can I wait 'til the shop shuts?"

"You can take me to the bus-stop, if you'd like that", my beloved spoke and said unto me, adding, smiling and, on the rising note that made it a question, "Love?"

I almost answered, "Rise up my love, my fair one, and come away", but said, instead: "Shall I wait here or at the door?"

"Here, if you like, Love", came her leg-pulling response. "I can see you better there, can't I?: see who else you're looking at, in here, isn't it?"

By the time that she'd waved me a laughing goodbye from the steps of the bus, she'd promised that we'd spend her "half-day off" together. "We'll go for a walk, is it?"

As the bus drew away, Cecil Parry rejoined me for our walk back to Trinity. He'd been with me when Cupid fletchered me. Good pal that he was, he'd taken himself off about his own business but not too far to lose touch, and he was as enthusiastic as I was about my sweet-counter encounter. What healthy Welshman could fail to be?

"We're meeting tomorrow", I said. "It's her half-day."

"Congratulations", said Cecil. "You're a lucky chap."

I wondered whether it was luck or fate and, anyway, Lord Beaverbrook had just written something about luck favouring "the prepared mind". My mind had been preparing for years for fate or fortune to smile on me in the way that that Princess of Pontyates had done from the step of her utility-bus "chariot of Amminadib".

"Do you think", asked my mentor, as we swung on to College Road, "that you should take things a bit easier when you meet her tomorrow?"

"What d'you mean?" said I – having had great difficulty in not running after that bus through Nott's Square – "easier?"

"Well! You know! Don't rush things. Give her time to get to know you. Take it easy: all the kissing an' all. You know, the other night, perhaps you were too eager."

I was stunned. If the sweet-counter had been narrower, I'd have had a go at kissing her in Woolworths. "Thy lips, O my spouse, drop as the honeycomb: honey and milk are under thy tongue" and I should put off tasting it?

"You mean, I shouldn't kiss her?" We'd already held hands at the bus-stop; she and I.

"Well, not tomorrow, anyway", said the wise young owl. "No need to rush it. Take your time with this girl. She's well worth it."

My mother had told me that I could do worse than listen to Cecil. Perhaps I'd take his advice. Perhaps I wouldn't.

On leaving home, I'd made a promise to Mam. "Promise me", she'd said, "that ewe'll read ewer Bible every night. Will ewe promise me that?" I did, and I had. Indeed, I kept the promise not only throughout the Trinity time but read a chapter every night for years after that. That sweet-counter encounter evening, there was no difficulty of choice. I read the love-letters of Solomon: "now also thy breasts shall be as clusters of the vine, and the smell of thy nose like apples; and the roof of thy mouth like the best wine for my beloved, that goeth down sweetly, causing the lips of those that are asleep to speak. I am my beloved's and his desire is towards me".

So let it be! Indeed it was. And, early the next afternoon, we walked together out of town, away from people, on to the winding, up-hill, A48 road that served then as the highway up to Swansea and to Cardiff and to London and, down below, to Neyland and, not wanting to go to any of these places, we turned off it, near the Tywi river bridge, into the byways.

I'd almost kissed her on meeting. She'd seemed ready to kiss me. Only, Cecil's voice, in the back of my mind, cautioned: "Take it easy: all the kissing an' all". So, I'd taken her hand instead and we'd walked close together – were even closer together now.

She was as lovely as King Solomon and I had remembered. Her glorious autumn hair, freed of work-day slides and grips, hung down in ringlets behind her all the way to her swinging hips. Chapter 7 said it all, from head to toe or, rather, from toe to head.

"How beautiful are thy feet with shoes" I might have quoted, because they were: greeting her with "O prince's daughter", because she progressed regally. "The joints of thy thighs are like jewels", I could have said, because her left thigh, rotating like a diamonded watch movement, was pacing and pulsing my right thigh preciously. Verses two, three and four, I'll leave to your researches, in case you should leave my book under your bed and it should fall into the hands of a minor. What about verses five and six, though, for a perfect parallel? "Thine head upon thee is like Carmel" – perhaps, given our original meeting place, "caramel" would have fitted too? – "and the hair of thine head like purple ... How fair and how pleasant art thou, O love, for delights". Solomon and Samuel (David Gordon Parry, that is) were in harmony with Sheba on the road to Llangunnor.

Delights there were already, simply in being with her. Pleasant she was and as teasing, as direct, as unusual, as at our first meeting. "You don't speak Welsh, do you, Love?" she asked. "There's a pity! Isn't it?" she said. She did, of course, and I had her say things to me in my native language that I could only understand in translation: lovely, lilting, lyrical, things, ending often in "Cariad", and I had no trouble with that. "Duw Cariad Yw" – "God is Love" – took me further back into my beginnings than that first Sunday of the war. The Queen of Sheba was calling me "Love" again, and I loved it. If Cecil Parry hadn't been bothering my head, I'd have taken her in my arms there and then and kissed her, gently. We made as if to do that, but I wasn't going to spoil it all. "Don't rush things", my Jiminy Cricket of a colleague whispered, subliminally, and I stepped back, even though she had stepped forward. She looked puzzled for a moment.

"Would you like to come home with me one day?" she asked after a while. "Meet my Mam an' Dad? Have tea in our house?"

I couldn't believe my fortune. "Do they know about me?" I questioned. "Have you told them about me, already?"

"Of course", she smiled. "We're like that, aren't we? our family. I'd told them about you, anyway – looking at all the other girls – before you looked at me. They'd like to meet you – especially now, isn't it? now that they know that your Dad is a Minister. They'll like that when I tell them, won't they Love? We're Chapel, too."

If ever there was a moment to kiss, it was then. I let it pass. What a damn' nuisance the keeper of my conscience was becoming.

I don't think that I could retrace our steps now, after all these years. We'd quit the secondary road quite early, making a left exit into a very much narrower one – little more than a lane – that led through pleached hazel hedges, up-hill, towards a Norman Church and churchyard. We were in the Parish of Llangunnor, and the gate of the churchyard was open to us. We sat down on a raised tomb, flat and warmed by the sun – and with dozens and dozens of tiny red money-spiders wandering at speed over it. I'd cochinealed such mites in their hundreds on similar slabs in the graveyard surrounding the cottage manse of my birth at Molleston. It was warm now. The church was open, too, and we'd walked around it, the only ones there. We could see to north, to south, to east and to west, and the far-away flocks of sheep – with some cattle, a mare and a leggy colt – that were the only living things but us on the whole of that green hill.

We sat a little apart. The princess of Pontyates had effected that. She had chosen to sit away from me, and for the first time since my blue eyes had locked with her amber ones, 24 hours before, there were other distances between us. She didn't reject my hand when I reached for hers but didn't move closer, either. What had I done that this remarkable girl was slipping away from me?

It was what I hadn't done, of course, what I hadn't been. In not being my own man – in marching to a different drum – I'd given the impression that I was reluctant to become involved in anything but in the most casual walk-about way with that marvellous girl. She'd been troubled by that.

Too late, I tried to make amends. As I turned my face to hers, she turned hers away from me. We were in the graveyard, alright, the graveyard of mutual attraction, of trust, of confidence, of high hopes.

I don't remember a great deal about the walk home. I do remember asking, "When shall I see you again?" I so much wanted to.

She said, "I'll write to you, is it? At the College?" but she didn't say "love" at the end of either question and my heart sank. What would her letter tell me that she couldn't tell me to my face?

That letter arrived in time for mid-morning break on the following Tuesday – one day before I had intended to lay siege on her at noon on Wednesday. Ironically, Cecil – who was sometimes handed all the Parry mail – gave it to me. "Your letter's come", he said. "You needn't have worried after all." There had, though, been every need.

Written, as I might have known it would be, in elegant script, it began, "Dear Gordon" but it was really a "Dear John" letter of the sort that departing wives, tired of waiting, wrote to their soldier husbands during the war.

She had, she said, thought about our meeting again but was now telling me that we shouldn't. She felt that there had been little real purpose in our time together. Mature as ever, she wrote kindly, wishing me well; but I was left believing that I'd failed her and failed myself. That night, the Song of Solomon had no comfort in it, and there was one verse that made me blush:

"I opened to my beloved; but my beloved had withdrawn himself and was gone. I sought him but I could not find him; I called him but he gave me no answer."

On the other hand, I could be rationalising all that in my own favour. I might just have bored the girl to death with all the talking, and tired her out with all the walking. I didn't buy Liquorice All-Sorts for months, and, when I did, she was gone. She was too beautiful for that sweet-counter, and Cecil Parry, wise though he was, had done me no favours. Since then, I've always tried to make my own mistakes.

I made none when I found myself, increasingly, turning my thoughts and fancies to the girls at home. At Milford, at Rosemarket, at the Jordanston Land Settlements and in Neyland itself, there were lovely friends who wrote to me while I was at Trinity. One, from Hakin, was really my first teenage sweetheart. Another, from Rosemarket, shared the sunlit summer of 1944 with me at Milton Bottoms and at Westfield Mill and beautiful it was – chasing but chaste, warm and wonderful – in the bracken above the full tide.

Towards the end of my time at College, three lovely daughters of Jack and Mary Incledon, Mavis, Glenys and Peggy, in the ascending order of their ages, became triple attractions, not simply for me but for most of my immediate group of Neyland lads. Mavis had lived among us the longest. Peggy was that subtle distance beyond us. Glenys not only wrote to me but – assisting her aunt in "Llewellyn's Cash Exchange" grocery store – sent me "under the counter" supplements to fill my half-biscuit tin. To a lad whose every appetite was alert and unrequited, the double-draw was irresistible. I've been married to Glenys for 47 of the 50 years since Trinity.

CHAPTER TEN

The Practice

There came a day when we stepped into a classroom. We had known from the beginning that we would. We were required to do two tranches of teaching during our time at Trinity. "Teaching Practice" took us to a chosen school where, for several weeks, we were supernumerary to the staff and – while the greater part of our time was spent "observing" them, noting their methods, their relationship with the classes that they taught, and general control – we were also expected to teach lessons.

In addition to the practice periods offered by the College, we were asked to arrange an attachment to one of our local, home schools for several weeks of the long summer vacation. Indeed, before going up to Trinity I had enjoyed a period of "observation" at one of Pembrokeshire's flag-ship schools, the newish central secondary school at Milford Haven.

Allocation of schools, for college teaching practice, was a matter for our tutors and overseen by Johnnie "Humph". In due time, a list of the allocations was posted on the Cloisters' notice-board. I found that I was to be practising at the town school that had actually been designed for the purpose, "The Model Practising School".

Its title foreshortened to "The Model School" or, even to "The Model", it was really two schools in one building but with rigidly apartheid lives; one was for boys and the other for girls. Their playgrounds were separated, too.

The Boys' School – and, as I came to believe, the whole Model set-up – was ruled by "Cheerful Charlie" Wilford. This lively Trinity man was here, there and everywhere, about his domain. Unusually for the headmaster of an unreorganised primary school, he wore his gown and carried his mortar-board headgear around with him. His every appearance was a performance and, standing in a doorway, saying nothing, gazing at the ceiling, he would bring quiet to the noisiest of classes.

Children seem to like a touch of pomposity in their teachers and they certainly love moments of drama. Mr. Wilford gave them both, trailing them around behind his flowing gown in an aura of excitement – a Pied Piper of the playground, the piano and the chalk-face.

Years later, Bryn Griffith – who, despite years of imprisonment by the Japanese in the notorious Changi Jail and of labour on the murderous mileage of the Bangkok to Siam railway, and despite desperate, chronic malarial attacks constantly debilitating him, was the most charismatic and inspired headmaster with whom I ever worked – told his staff members, gathering for a briefing on the day before we were all to welcome the 900 pupils into the new County Secondary School at Haverfordwest: "Whatever support you need in any circumstances arising in your classes, you will find me on your side but, if you bore your pupils, you'll be on your own."

Charlie Wilford would have shouted "Amen!" to that. He was what my mother would have called "Full, the place", overflowing with energy and enthusiasm in a school that couldn't have changed very much since Forster's influence led the Church to re-provision it.

The Girls' School was headed by the sister of the ubiquitous Dean of St. Davids. She, unlike her powerful brother, was comfortable with life as she found it. Her influence, her personality, made for quiet that didn't need dramatic demonstrations of strength in the doorway. She had around her, too, a smallish staff of like-minded ladies. Perhaps it was in that first teaching practice, at that Model Girls' school, that I began to understand the vital and subtle difference between imposing discipline upon others and bringing it out from them. When the Notice Board showed me that I'd been nominated to practise at a girls' school, I'd been startled.

Later, I discovered that my name had played its part in that. Sending a Parry to a Parry was a bit of an in-house joke but, when I met the lady, she confessed that she had been amused and interested to see that we shared a surname: were we related?

No, we weren't. Our Parrys had come only lately to West Wales. Nor could I go much further back into the history of our Ap Harris than my grandfather. We did, though, get on very well together from our first meeting. Apprehensive, on crossing the playground that morning, moving among groups of girls rang-ing in age from fourish to fourteen plus, I had given a quite unintentional Charlie Wilford quietus to the games going on before bell-time. Everything had stopped for my progress. It was flattering, really. I enjoyed it.

You must remember that I was eighteen-years-old, less than four years older than the oldest girls, but their reactions made me feel very grown-up and important. As I passed, the individuals and groups came back to life in my wake.

"He's our Studie", I heard one of the girls say, pronouncing it "Stew-dee-a" with that elongation of the original vowel into a second one that was, then, and is, still, an attractive decoration of the Carmarthen English of bilingual children. I remember that the younger ones flocked around their "Stew-dee-a" as he reached the school door. Some of them had their hands high in the air.

"Sir!" "Sir!" "Sir!" they shouted. "Can I tell Miss that ewer 'ere, Sir?" It was the very first time in my life that anyone had called me "Sir", and I had every right to savour it. There was, though, no need for anyone to tell "Miss" that I was there. She had seen me coming, and, most graciously, appeared on the doorstep at that very moment to welcome me.

Now was the time for me to find out if there was a teacher in me. It was the time for the College to find that out, too. The system was geared to it. It had grown naturally out of the earlier "pupil-teacher" structures that, for many years, had allowed promising people – usually the brighter sons and daughters of "the working classes" – to further their own education by remaining in the standardised schools, moving from Standard Seven into Standard "X" Seven and, from there, taking up monitoring duties, giving support, in return for their own after-school tuition, to the headmaster, who was often the only qualified teacher at the school. Almost apprentices to him, they would, ultimately, emerge as uncertificated teachers. They would, often, have had the support, too, of the scholarship of vicars and curates who would give them "in-service education" in the classics, in the scriptures, and in the elements of philosophy.

The talent that was recruited in this way has not, perhaps, been given the credit that it deserves. Only a generation away from my own, these "pupil teachers" were, even in retirement, reinforcing the systems and standards of our democracy. Surprisingly – even astonishingly – well educated, given their limited

Miss Leggat's Class: Neyland Infants Schools, 1929.
Gordon John; Chris Harvey; Mervyn Phillips; Iris Lloyd; Teddy Bevan; May Sutch; Gordon Parry.
Hughie Warlow; Joan Llewellyn; Tommy Larkin; Maisie McCormac; Gerald Myers; Gloria Morris; Letty Spall; Ivor Lloyd.
Joey Woolridge; Cathleen Davies; Peggy Spall; Peggy Hall; Glenis Davies.

exposure to any sort of full-time tuition, they read and they wrote and they conversed, conveying, transferring, their own appetites for learning to the children of their day. Reading, 'Riting and 'Rithmetic were their strengths.

Sadly, there was really no "Tom Brown's Schooldays" of the public education system. Growing out of private patronage, consolidating itself through the Church Schools into a national, if parochial – variable in quality and quantity – matrix of opportunity and, then, by legislation and the Board Schools, putting itself, first, within reach, and, ultimately, making itself mandatory for all children, it didn't find its own Thomas Hughes to do it literary justice – or to engender respect and affection for it on the Rugby School scale. Perhaps Emlyn Williams meant to do so in "The Corn Is Green" and his autobiography, "George", but fell short. As a result, the limitations of the system tend to be remembered, while its triumphs are understated, if not forgotten.

Possibly because I'd never really left school myself, going – with the shortest of summer breaks – from a sixth-form to a college run like a sixth-form, and with the Carmarthen primary school classrooms replicating my own first schools at "The Infants" and at "The Boys' School" in John Street, Neyland, I was immediately at ease in "The Model Girls".

For an end-of-the-century, eve-of-the-new millennium, reader, I should write, here, of my own beginnings in public education. Our home, 15 John Street, faced the cluster of three – at first, unconnected – buildings that made up the Board School provision for the town in 1929. Within days of our moving in to Bethesda's terraced manse, I was sent off across the road to "The Infants".

Children began school early, then, and I was three years and nine months old when I did so. Even at 70 years of age, I can recall the drama and the disaster of it all.

My brother Bryn, seven years older than I was, had left home hours earlier. By the rigid rules of the times, having sat for "scholarship" entry to Narberth Grammar School, while we lived at Molleston, he was obligated to complete one academic year there before transferring to Pembroke Dock. This involved that eleven-year-old boy's rising in the deep dark of the autumn mornings, eating a solitary breakfast, in front of our kitchen fire, making the 1,000 yards walk to Neyland pontoon, boarding the 7.00 a.m. ferry, crossing the estuary to Hobb's Point, walking at least half a mile along the Pier Road, up Water Street, over the level crossing, into Hawkston Road, entering the railway station, boarding the 8.00 a.m. train and riding in it to Narberth station, demounting and walking a little distance still to arrive in time for registration, assembly, and a day's lessons before unwinding all of that route again to be home by 6.30 p.m. A long way and a long day for a first-former in rain, wind, sunshine and snow-time – it would have taxed an adult.

Our sister Hilda was luckier than he. The oldest of us, she had completed enough time at Narberth to transfer directly to Pembroke Dock. She had left John Street that morning, as every morning, to catch the 8.00 a.m. ferry.

Mary, the sister who was five years older than I, had begun to attend the "Girls' School", immediately opposite our front-door and had already joined her friends in the yard.

I stood on our front doorstep, loathe to leave it even to cross the chequered tiles to the iron gate of the narrow forecourt. My father and my mother were close behind me, between the glass-door and the storm-door, encouraging me to cast off and make my way out into life.

"Go ewe along, now, like a good boy; there's a good boy!" said Mam, gently, with a firm hand in the small of my back, propelling me from tile to tile – a pawn on a chessboard.

"Off you go, Boy", said Dad. "There's Ritchie Davies coming."

Ritchie Davies was, indeed, on his way, but he had his sisters on either side of him for solace. I was alone, wobbling on the edge of the nest, fearful of solo flight.

Eventually, I cast off. I crossed the road slowly, reluctantly, intent on intercepting Ritchie and having some company through the forbidding, spikey, school gate. Almost at the other pavement, I turned to see if my parents were still there. Reassured that they were, I took one more step without taking my eyes off Mam and Dad.

It was then that disaster struck me, or, rather, it was then that I struck disaster. I walked smack into Bertie Snow's red lamp-post and sank, semi-conscious, to the gutter. When I came round, I was back in our kitchen, laid out on our "chaise-longue", scroll-ended, single-armed, sofa, with my head wrapped around with vinegar-soaked brown paper tied with string.

My parents cossetted and comforted me through the morning, as an egg of a bump waxed and waned on my temple. The brown-paper came off. Golden butter went on. I began to smell like fish and chips. Mafeking had been relieved for me, but not for long. I rose to sit at the table for Monday lunch – cold left-overs from Sunday's roast beef and Yorkshire pudding – and, by 1.30 p.m., I was back on the doorstep again. My giant stride had been postponed but not cancelled. In a little while, I was seated, for the first time, in the class of Miss Carrie Leggat.

Dr. Spock – the American Psychologist, not the Vulcan – had no hold on the minds of our parents or our teachers. His damage was yet to be done. So, there I was. I'd been comforted but not indulged; cared for but not "spoiled"; bruised but not broken. I was a schoolboy, already, and it was 1929.

Miss Carrie Leggat, an uncertificated teacher herself, had all the modern teaching aids available to help her to set us on the official road to learning. Chief among these were slates, slate pencils, and a box of silver sand.

Yes! We learned our letters by tracing them in sand with our fore-fingers. First, the slate monitors would deliver the heavy, wood-framed slates to us at our places. Then, the sand monitor would come to pour fine sand on to the slates up to the level of the wooden surround. Later, biggish for my age, I became a slate monitor, but the honour of pouring sand eluded me.

Some of us served as ink monitors, as pencil monitors, as wet-rag and water carriers for "wiping the slate clean" at the end of a lesson. Sayings that are in use every day had their origins in the practices of classrooms such as Carrie Leggat's. There was "starting with a clean slate", "following the top line", "turning over a new leaf" in our exercise books, and all long before education came to be shaped by "the bottom line" of the Schools' Funding Council.

At the "Infants", and at "the big boys' school" next door, I'd been well prepared for my first morning at Miss Parry's academy. My gentle introduction to practising to be a teacher, there, comes back to me in comfortable memories.

Chief among these is the reception given, by staff and pupils, when I spoke to the entire school in what was meant to be a lesson on health and hygiene. I'd hit on the idea of using a toy telephone, complete with a ringing dialling tone, as a body cell. The lesson consisted of sending various messages to the brain and reactions to them, in movements of arms and legs, by the body. It had been fun to prepare and was fun on the day. I was –

to complete the analogy – finding my feet in the classroom, and visiting tutors who sat in on the other efforts of mine were helpful.

When we went down for the summer vacation, my father – as Chairman of the Pembrokeshire Education Committee – arranged for me to do further practising at the Milford Haven Central School. In a fine, modern building, set in its own grounds and playing-fields, it had a locally famous and highly respected headmaster, Mr. "Boss" Phillips. The staff was as good as its Head, and to be allowed to be with some of them was a privilege. I made friendships in the clubby atmosphere of the "apartheid" male staff-room of that co-educational school that have – in several cases – lasted through until now. One friend made there earlier, and a friend still, was a former Trinity student, Mr. Ralph Llywelyn. He had recruited me to the Army Cadet Force and added the dimension of a Summer camp at Aberaeron to my already exciting life, improving my chances of eventually winning a post in Pembrokeshire.

My second, College-based period of practice took me further afield. I had hoped to go back to the "Model". I had, in fact, been told by a member of the staff whom I'd met in the Market that I was going back – "a special request from Miss Parry for her namesake" she'd said. In the event, it was Cecil Parry who responded to the call. "Sam" Parry was sent to Old Road School, Llanelli. It wasn't the Gulag Archipelago, not outer Siberia, but it wasn't what I'd been anticipating, and my time there began in frost and icy mornings.

To get to Llanelli in time for morning school presupposed an extra early rising. I well recall leaving the Wing in pre-Bell darkness, negotiating the Jacob's ladder of the stairway down to the Cloisters, and lining up for breakfast with a couple of dozen colleagues who were allocated to schools from Cwmffrwd to Llanelli. It was even cold in the kitchen at that hour. The dining-room was freezing. We knew what to expect outside.

Outside, too, was that utility bus or its "ringer". Inside the bus, there were no lights. We groped our way aboard. My overcoat was one of the Co-op's best – cheap but substantial – and belted in the trench-coat fashion mimicry of the day. My scarf was tied around my head and chin, and tucked into my collar. Climbing aboard, I'd left a little cloud of my half-ounce bacon-breath frozen in the morning air. The air in the bus was frozen, too, scything the upper reaches of my nostrils and tightening the soft palate and the tonsils at the back of my mouth. I remembered the quinine initiation of my first week.

We were an unusually subdued bus-full for a college trip but, then, we didn't trip too often in the dark before dawn of a winter day. The bus seemed to be out before its time, too, coughing and spitting as it pulled away from the steps at the Wing door.

At the gate, it turned up-hill rather than down, following the rising left-hand curve of the road to pass the front gates of the Asylum and the back entrance to Trinity before dropping downhill towards the junction with the A48 and turning left. It was still too dark to see the towering Picton monument except as a silhouette against the eastern sky. Skirting the outskirts of the town, we took the bridge over the Tywi, before turning on to the secondary A484 that would take us into Llanelli.

This was newish territory for me, perhaps the first time that I ever rode that road. As yet, there was, still, only a little light, but the day was dawning. I knew the main places along the way but only as seen from the windows of railway-train carriages. I looked forward to passing through them.

We would stop at most of those places, dropping off students scheduled to serve out their main practice of their course at the primary schools en route. Someone dismounted in near-darkness at Llandefaelog. Several more were on the bus doorstep ready to step down at Kidwelly. It was light enough there for the castle to loom out of the gloom. I believe that we'd delivered to school gates at Ferryside and Llansaint, too, swinging out towards the coast and back along the Gwendraeth to take up the A484 again under the castle walls. There were students for schools at Pembrey and we glimpsed the war, lurking in the shadows of the R.A.F. fighter base, on the flat lands between Trimsaran and the sea.

Out there, on the levels, it was nearing sun-rise and, already, the eastern sky was aureating, gilding itself, glowing golden but with the fires of the furnace in it.

The utility bus was running west to east, now, and the rising sun was presenting itself, raising a rim, an aureole, a radiance, about the heads of the lower foothills running to the sea from the Black Mountains. The shoreline of Cefn Padrig and the wider sweep of the Loughor estuary welcomed the sea on a highish tide and – out there, on its headland – Llanelli waited to welcome us, though very few there knew that we were on our way and even fewer of those would have been stirred by the knowledge.

This was wartime Llanelli. Production for war had given it renewed vitality. It had come back into its own out of the despondency and neglect of the inter-war "depression". Its factories, its furnaces, its surrounding collieries, were straining to contribute to the war effort. There was full employment and – as is the way with foundries, furnaces and collieries – chimney stacks and washeries pumped waste products into the sky night and day.

It was the filtering of the rays of the rising sun through the saturation of chemicals and motes and flecks of suspended solids in the lower sky that – not only that morning but that evening and every rising and setting of the sun throughout our teaching time in Llanelli – made a breathless beauty out of a grim and grimy industrial landscape, scarred and cicatrised by the failures of the past.

In the half-century since that first journey to Old Road School, Llanelli, I've travelled the world. Only the Arctic, Antarctica and South America are unvisited by me. I've swum in five out of the seven seas, and seen the sun rise over the "tourist traps" of north, south, east and west. Yet, never anywhere have I seen such colours and lights, such an aurora borealis of the sky, as attended our every morning run to Llanelli in 1944.

Old Road School itself was not beautiful, but its reputation was good. The reputation of its headmaster was even better. Mr. Morgan, a graduate of distinction, a local historian, writer and public man, welcomed us on arrival. There was little fuss. The atmosphere was friendly. He told us about his school building, his scholars and his general attitude to Trinity students and their teaching practice. He introduced us to his staff and told us which of them would be hosting us and in which classrooms.

My supervising teacher was the oldest member of staff. He was, in fact, so old that, in peace-time, he would have been long retired. Indeed, he'd been called back out of retirement and cheerfully admitted to me that he was as old then as I am now – nudging 70! So many young male teachers had been called up – ultimately, fit men of up to 36-years-old were being conscripted – that education authorities sought qualified, time-served teachers from their retirement lists to help keep schools running.

Mr. Watts's looks and energy belied his years. I found him fascinating from day one. For years, he had lived and worked in South Africa. He was quick to tell me all about that because, as he said: "There's a good part of me still out there. In my heart, I miss Jo'burg more than I can say." Student of advanced geography though I was, I had to tell him that I'd never heard of Jo'burg. "Yes, you have!" he said. "Of course you have! Jo'burg is Johannesburg, South Africa's largest city. Everybody calls it Jo'burg there."

During the next weeks, I was to be given a running seminar on its evolution, over a hundred years, from a gold mining camp into the financial and commercial hub of the prosperous Witwatersrand, and of the life-style enjoyed by the white citizens.

I learned of the less than adequate lives led by non-whites; of the "Cape coloured" Asians and their suburb of Lenasia. "They are doing the same job for South Africa – running businesses and such – as the Jews did in medieval Europe," he told me. "Hard-working, intelligent, industrious, they won't be in the suburbs for ever."

Mr. Watts talked, too, of the South West Townships of Johannesburg, "Where the blacks live in vast numbers on the extreme south-west limits of the city". Just as he had abbreviated Johannesburg to Jo'burg, he abbreviated South West Townships to Soweto. It was the first time that I'd heard of that, too, and I wonder when we shall hear the last of it?

Even more fascinating than that was this doyen's artistry. Seeing some drawings of mine illustrating points in my prepared lesson notes, Mr. Watts was kind and encouraging. I liked to draw, and he claimed that he liked what I'd drawn.

"My great relaxation", he told me, "is drawing and painting. I'll bring some of my sketch-books in, if you like."

When he did, I resolved never to show him any drawings of mine ever again. His work was magnificent. Dozens and dozens of drawing-pads – pocket-sized and plain-covered – contained pictures of landscapes that he'd painted both in South Africa and in South Wales. About halfway through his collection, colour ceased to feature in his work.

"I tired of it, you know?" he said. "Was keener on the draughtsmanship. Began to concentrate on shades of black and white. Liked the results; not so fleeting as colour somehow. Funny, isn't it? An old man from Jo'burg giving up colour, going in for black and white."

What a find that man was! What an education, over and above education, he gave me! My teaching practice leapt into new dimensions. What a nonsense, too, that man's presence in that wartime school makes of buying teachers prematurely out of service in their early fifties and of introducing financial funding that obliges headteachers to appoint two newly-qualified, inexperienced assistants rather than have them afford one qualified, experienced one at the top of the scale. Isn't there danger in staffing our schools with the ingénues and heading them with the menopausal, of either sex?

I even experienced a moment of embarrassment that makes my point. At break-time and in the dinner hour, Mr. Watts and I joined the other staff who were not on playground duty. There was only one other male member of that staff. He was just about old enough to have missed conscription but had been everywhere, seen everything and, when he spoke, he expected no dog to bark. There came a day when what he was saying seemed so ridiculous that I barked.

"Well!", said I, with all the temerity of youth. "That's not been my experience."

The man looked at me as though I'd crawled out from under a stone. I was conscious of the bemused – perhaps amused – expressions of the lady members of staff and began to regret my intervention.

Sir Oracle drew himself up to his full 5 foot 6 inches. His chest puffed out. Some of his stomach was drawn in. Then from that lofty height, he said: "Your experience! Your experience! What experience have you had at eighteen, may I ask? I've had 20 years' experience in the classroom." With all the monstrous pomposity of onsetting middle-age, the older bull – full of the stuff that older bulls are full of – was determined to crush the young bull before his status in the herd was threatened. He succeeded. I blushed and said no more. Mercifully, the bell went.

As Mr. Watts walked with me back to his classroom, he put a comforting arm about my shoulder. "Don't let him upset you, Parry, boy", he said. "Take no notice. That clown hasn't had 20 years' experience in the classroom."

"Hasn't he?" I asked. "He said he has."

"Yes! I know that he said he had, but he hasn't. He's only had ONE year's experience but the bugger's had it TWENTY TIMES."

You can understand, now, why I remember that delightful man. He helped me draw up lesson notes, suggested references and illustrations, and stood back in his own classroom, to give me space to grow in confidence there. We shared a moment of real delight one morning.

The class was mixed. Its pupils were young; in their second year at primary school. There was one lad who had a small problem. It caught up with him one cold morning. I'd assumed that a tiny trickling noise was coming from a tap somewhere. A blue-eyed child, with curls and ribbons, thought that I should know the truth. Her hand shot into the air.

"Please, Sir! Please, Sir!" she said, anxiously. "David Lewis 'as left the room on the floor, Sir!"

Rescuing David from his puddle of piddle without embarrassing him further was a delicate business, especially as neither his teacher nor I dared laugh at Margaret's delicate announcement.

I don't really remember the detail of my final lesson, the one observed by Vice-Principal Humphreys and, for some reason, a new tutor in Rural Science. I was surprised because Mr. J. B. Jones didn't teach me. An early environmentalist, he might have been there because I had chosen to refer to the life of the ant.

Mr. Humphreys had reviewed my notes with me during an earlier visit. My choice of topic had surprised him, then, as much as it does me, now. "You're not going to tell them to go to the ant, thou sluggard, are you, Parry?" he asked. "You know, your father and the pulpit? Might be a bit heavy for Standard 2." I had been going to, but I denied it.

Cecil Parry's father – a dockyard joiner and craftsman – had been working for weeks on a mahogany and perspex panelled model of an artesian well for Cecil's final lesson at the Model Girls. A model fit for the Model, layered in clay and porous stone, it sent up a fountain when water was poured into it. It made my cardboard ant look a bit shabby.

Come the day – an icy cold one – everyone rallied round. The class, determined to help, was unnaturally natural. Mr. Watts was Mr. Watts. Mr. Morgan and his staff made Johnnie "Humph" and his colleagues welcome, helping to relax them, and I, in due course, launched into the lesson. While the Vice-Principal was tucked away at the back of the room, Mr. Jones killed two birds with one stone: perhaps that should be "one stove".

The room was heated by an open coal-fire. There was an iron guard, half-barrel shaped, around it. Earlier, it had been sleeting outside. Mr. Jones, sporting a winter-weight Harris Tweed suit, had chosen to step inside the fire-guard to dry the damp out of his trouser legs and to observe me more closely from the front of the room.

Mine must have been an absorbing lesson. My cardboard ant must have been better than I thought. No-one in the class noticed – until the Rural Scientist hurdled out from the fire-place, kicking over the guard in transit – that his Harris tweeds were on fire.

"Go thee to the ant thou sluggard", indeed! There was nothing sluggardly about our burnt-offering novitiate. Tweed doesn't flame, it melts. Happily, Mr. Jones was wearing Long Johns under his trousers. His legs were hot, hot, hot, but they hadn't burned. Someone came and took him away for cooling and changing. Soon afterwards, my final teaching practice lesson came to an end.

Bryn Griffith would have been proud of me. The ant and the fire-place antics had left no-one bored that day. The tutors were kind to me. They saw the makings of a teacher in me, and marked me accordingly. Cecil Parry and his father's artesian well earned an "A". All the Parrys were pleased with themselves. Keeping up with the Joneses is always a challenge!

It was with real regret that I left Old Road School, Llanelli. It was with even greater regret that I said goodbye to the artist – philosopher – teacher, who taught me so much. I do hope that his sketch-books are preserved on display somewhere in Llanelli. Mr. Watts had been in the habit of capturing the same local scene, over and over again, in varying lights. Using, finally, only black-on-white to bring the changes, for differing times of the day, his life-time hobby is part of the heritage of the town. "Practice makes perfect", he told me. "One day, I might get there."

In that rackety utility bus, I wasn't the only Trinity student to look back over his shoulder beyond Pwll to see for one more time the winter dusk building behind the industrial skyline. Perhaps, though, I was the only one that evening to see it all in black and white. "Practice makes perfect", I thought. "One day, I might get there."

That thought, in those words, must, constantly, have been in the mind and strengthening the purpose of Flight Sergeant J. A.

Davies of Boncath. Right then, he was further from home than ever. After several identity changes, from Belgian peasant to Dutch farm-hand, to being "a young man expensively attired in blue sport shirt, felt hat, new suit and new shoes", he had been routed south by his "underground" helpers, travelling first-class, on forged papers, through the South Netherlands, through Belgium and into France. It was a roundabout road to Boncath, and there were thousands of miles yet to go. One day, though, he would get there.

CHAPTER ELEVEN

The Times

Our first full month in Trinity had coincided with a dramatic change in the fortunes of World War Two. Joe Davies, the coalman, had been right. Our enemies had begun, during early 1943, to retreat and, very largely – despite occasional setbacks – they were retreating to "our bloody plan, now, Boss", all over the place: "If you'll forgive the language, Ma'am".

During the first week of January, the German armies went into retreat in the Caucasus and along the Valley of the Don. By the 18th, the slaughterous sixteen-month siege of Stalingrad ended. On the 23rd, the Eight Army recaptured Tripoli and, while American bombers were making their first night attacks on the German homeland, the remnants of Hitler's army around Stalingrad surrendered.

In February, the U.S. services drove the Japanese out of Guadalcanal Island, seven days before the Russians retook their city of Kharkov.

In March and in May, there were Allied victories everywhere. Tunis and Bizerta fell on 7th May, and the Germans gave up the fight in Tunisia by the 16th. Four days after that, the Royal Air Force breached the Mohn and Eder dams in the Ruhr valley and drowned thousands and thousands. It was that sort of war. There was so much dying everywhere that drowning cities and citizens was seen as heroic. Barnes-Wallis's "Bouncing Bombs" were a rather amusing British "trick". Undeniably, the men who flew them in and dropped them were heroic airmen by any standards, and the "justification" was the damage that the man-made floods would do to the war products of the "Forge of Germany".

While I was working at Penblwyn, Barn Street, Haverfordwest, for the Pembrokeshire War Agricultural Executive, safe, comfortable, looking forward to being a student, on 19th July, the Allies invaded Sicily. As we've marked already, by 3rd September and my first full College day, the Italian mainland had been invaded.

For the next two years, our alarms and excursions – the daily round, the common task – took place almost in isolation from the momentous changes that were redrawing the map of Europe and forging power-blocks out of shattered nations that would dictate the future for half a century. The world was being refashioned. Trinity College, essentially, stood apart from it.

Peripherally, we were all at war. There were pre-service units such as the University Air Squadron. There was an Officers Training Corps, or was it the Home Guard? We spent whole nights on a "Fire Watching" rota; on duty in a small room beside the Fives Courts at the side of the Examination Hall. Actually, we played Fives – belting a small India-Rubber ball about with our bare hands – long into the light nights, and at dawn, far enough from the Wing not to disturb anyone with our endless tamping.

By the drizzling dark of November, with British troops and their allies well into France and heading for the Low Countries, with the Russians advancing on Kiev, and the Americans winning the Second Battle of the Solomons, the three most powerful men in the world, Churchill, Roosevelt and Stalin, took themselves off – two days before my 18th birthday – to Teheran. There it seems, they set programmes in motion to speed the end of the Second World War. It seems likely, too, that suspicions arising among them, there, signalled the "Cold War" that was to break out before the hot one was over.

As we were thinking Christmas in Trinity, there was disturbing news for young men on deferred service from the military. Most of us were looking forward to being called up. Inside our own heads, we rather hoped that they'd keep the war going until we could prove what heroes we were. I had a taste for uniform myself and, since the "declaration", I'd worn the blue overalls and tam-o'-shanter of an Auxiliary Fire Service messenger-boy; swopped those for a similar set and rôle in the Air Raid Precautions' service; added the uniform and stripes of a corporal in the Neyland Detached Flight of the Milford Haven Squadron of the Air Training Corps to my wardrobe; transferred, temporarily, into the khaki of the Army Cadet Force, going off to camp in Aberaeron, wearing the yellow-shoulder-bars of an Under-Officer, for a glorious week playing soldiers and chasing girls on the sandy shores and river-banks of Ceredigion; and had, in September,

1943, hoped to be in the U.A.S., the University Air Squadron, white "air crew" flash in my cap and all.

I saw myself, as I've said, as a fighter pilot, charging through the skies, shouting, "Tally-ho! Bogies! Give 'em hell, chaps!" and covering myself with glory and medal ribbons. Suddenly, another prospect reared. Heroic, in its own way, its appeal to me was limited. On the 2nd December, it was announced that men aged between 18 and 25 could be directed to serve their country in the coal-mines. A cock-pit was one thing, a coal-pit wholly another.

The coalition war-time Minister of Labour from 1940 to 1945 was the man who had been "The Dockers' K.C." and had later become General Secretary of the Transport and General Workers' Union, Ernest Bevin. By 1943, miners were needed as much as soldiers, sailors and airmen. Coal won wars as much as bullets did. Bevin brought in legislation to conscript young miners. They became the "Bevin Boys" and served heroically. I recall that some Trinity students did.

Poverty had conscripted generations of Parrys to cut coal. My father had escaped from the coal-pit to the pulpit. It would have been a reversal of recent family history if I'd been sent down one. Many were.

There was, by the way, a very relevant sequel to the high-summer, school-boy "soldiering", the dancing and romancing of that Army Cadet Force week in Aberaeron. I'd met a sun-burned girl in a dance, at the sea-port's community hall, who was more than first among equals. We'd been close for the free-time of the rest of the week and sworn to keep in touch. Settling in to Trinity, very soon afterwards, I was approached by one of my seniors. He introduced himself as W. G. Roach and carried friendly messages to me from my August-in-Aberaeron friend, who had been at school with him in Ceredigion. I was delighted and had every intention of responding warmly and affectionately. But I was caught-up in a new life, in a new place. Trinity College had taken me over, and I didn't: so many roads, so many good intentions!

Months later, the gentlemanly W. G. Roach sought me out again. "Sam", he said, "you slipped up badly by not keeping in-touch. Your friend's father has just won a fortune on the Football Pools!"

And there was a sequel to the sequel! Later still, I was told that the kindly messenger, W. G. Roach, was one of the first ex-students of Trinity to be called-up to be a "Bevin Boy" and to do his war service cutting coal.

As Warwick Taylor says in his book *The Forgotten Conscript: A History of the Bevin Boys*, "The Government failed to recruit enough school-leavers for the pits and in December, 1943, decided that 50,000 miners had to be recruited in 18 months."

Would you believe that, years and years later than any of that, there was a sequel to the sequel to the sequel? When I was Chairman of the Wales Tourist Board, I hosted a function for the "movers and shakers" of Wales. Among the guests was the "first citizen" of a sea-side authority, wearing about her shoulders the chain of an office that, for so long, was almost wholly kept for men. Her Worship was my sun-burned-summer-girl of 1943 and, very briefly and very publicly – 40 years on from our adolescence – we held hands again and glimpsed an unpaved road beside the Aeron. Aren't we lucky that Wales is so compact, so comfortable, a country?

You might find it difficult to imagine that, back in College for a fortnight of the new term by the end of January, 1944, we should still be largely isolated from the massive events laying waste to continental Europe. We were – at Trinity – an "island" on a peninsula that was itself attached to an off-shore island. Literally, we were cloistered there. The wireless; the shrunken, wartime newspapers; letters from home and friends, brought us news from the outside world. If they hadn't done, we would scarcely have known that other Mafekings were being relieved. The wireless, by the way, even in "portable" form, was housed in a largish box, was expensive, and not something that your average student had with him at College.

The Anzio landings; Argentina's break with the Axis; American forces moving into the Marshal Islands; Russians entering Estonia; the controversial Allied bombing and obliteration – despite the pleadings of the Vatican – of the sacred Monte Casino, in Italy, occupied as Rome had been, by the German Army, all occurring during the Spring Term, scarcely intruded into our routines.

It was all speeding up, though. The Battle for Rome began and ended. The King of Italy abdicated and, two days later, on the 6th June, we entered the Examination Hall, after breakfast, to sit our First Year "Finals".

We had scarcely begun the paper of that morning – I believe

Chairman of the Wales Tourist Board, Lord Parry, introducing a new policy document, stands at the roadside above Pontypool

that it was an English Literature one – when the old warrior, Captain Ithel Thomas, entered, looking flustered with excitement. He had a quick and contagious word with our invigilator, Dai Griff, who jumped to his feet, excited, too.

"Gentlemen!" Captain Ithel Thomas, T.D., shouted. "Gentlemen, Please! You'll forgive my interrupting you when you hear my news!"

There was a pause. We put down our pens and brought our minds back out of concentration.

"Gentlemen! I have to tell you that it has just been announced that, at dawn this morning, Allied forces landed on the beaches of Normandy. A massive invasion of the nearer continent has begun. The Second Front has been extended into France. Let's give three cheers: "Hip-hip-hip!" he shouted. We yelled, "Hooray!" "Hip-hip-hip!" We yelled "Hooray!" again. "Hip-hip-hip!" and, for the third time, we rang the rafters.

"Thank you, gentlemen", said the diminutive patriot. "Thank you very much, and the best of luck with your examinations."

It was D-Day, out there. Somewhere, along the beaches of Normandy, support planes were death-diving as the 4,000 ships of the invasion fleet ferried men to live or to die in "the longest day" that, already, had been terminally, painfully short for thousands.

The juddering, shattering, battering bombardment from offshore naval guns, the cascading bombs, the throbbing engines, the screaming bullets and ricocheting shrapnel, of attack and counter-attack, shook and slaughtered the sea-shore, and we contributed three, hearty cheers to the murderous, suicidal din of war from our island of calm in Carmarthen.

Then we settled back from that battle of 1944 to the blank-versed heroics of Henry IV, Part One, turning our attention to the battle at Shrewsbury, in 1403.

Later, I learned that Glenys Incledon, my friend and "grey-market" rations provider, had before dawn, that D-Day morning, played her own part in winning the war. As did almost everyone, Glenys had taken on "a war effort" extra job. She had become a night-time telephone operator at the Neyland Post Office run by Mr. "Gladdie" Gladwin Harries. Reporting to the Post-Master several evenings a week, she womanned – we used to say manned – the manual switchboard overnight. On the 5th of June, Mr. Harries had special "hush-hush" instructions for her. He gave her a "Private, Confidential, Official Secret" list of telephone numbers.

"I've set my alarm clock for 4 a.m.", he said. "You won't be on your own, but we'll have important work to do."

Over the previous months, Pembrokeshire had become a khaki county. There were many more troops than its civil population based there. Neyland itself had no space with a roof on it that didn't house soldiers or service equipment. Two splendid green-heart wooden piers had been built out from the Park and Picton Road beaches into the deeper water of the estuary. The beaches themselves had been surfaced with acres of concrete "chocolate blocks".

Everyone in Neyland knew that these piers and their approaches were for loading tanks, lorries, guns, soldiers, on to troop-carrying ships and landing-craft for the much-demanded "Second Front". There had even been a disastrous rehearsal for it when rough tides off the south Pembrokeshire beaches and unstable landing-craft had drowned unknown numbers of young Americans at Amroth, Freshwater West and Castlemartin.

At Trinity, we were still answering examination papers when, next day, the combined Indian armies beat off the Japanese from their sub-continent and our exams were still on, when, on the 9th of June, my Uncle Harold Parry, my father's youngest brother, one of his twelve brothers and sisters, won the Military Medal in the battle for Caen. Before the week was out, determined to distract the remorseless advance into Europe, Germany had launched its first "V-1" rocket – "the doodling, buzz-bomb" – on England. In South Wales, examinations were over, and life went on quietly. Uncle Harold was decorated "for valour" on the battlefield, by General Sir Bernard Montgomery, and I have the photograph to prove it.

As for me, I had two extraordinary pieces of luck with Henry IV, Part One. On the evening before the English Literature exam, I'd taken a break. Because others obviously were, I'd done some studying for the Literature paper. I liked the subject and enjoyed "Llew" Llewellyn's lectures. I'd nipped out for a shower and shampooed my hair, relaxing, scrunched up in the pediment basin of the shower, flat on my back with my feet in the air. Making my way back with my locks lank with dripping water, I'd planned to dry myself off in my room. En route, I stuck my damp head in through Cecil Parry's doorway.

"How's the swotting going?" I asked.

"All right", he said. "Just finishing 'Henry IV, Part One'."

"Part what?" I asked, my spirits sinking. "Henry, the who?"

The news was as bleak as I'd feared. It was on our syllabus. I'd never opened it. First, I had to find it. It was hard to find, hidden away in my fibre suitcase, under my bed. I would have climbed on to the bed to read it but my head was still dripping shower water.

You remember that we had a table and a chair furnishing each room? Over the table was an ingenious electric lamp. It was easily adjustable, on a brass chain, fairly heavily weighted with a metal "egg". You could raise it into the ceiling or lower it to touch the table-top.

Had it been a year later, I would have learned from the roasting of the environmentalist, Mr. J. B. Jones, the dangers of trying to kill two birds with one warm stone. I opened the Shakespeare play on the table, took a towel from the wash-basin rail and arranged it around the lamp-shade. Sitting on the chair, I lowered the lamp until my head was comfortably under the towel, with my hair warming to the lamp bulb, and got my mind down to the doings of Hotspur, Hal and Falstaff.

I'd barely begun when I was hit by a blinding light. It wasn't a revelation of the rebellion of the Percys, the Douglases, Mortimer or Glendower, or intellectual lightning dramatising the Shrewsbury victory of Hal, the Prince of Wales, or of Falstaff feigning death. It was an electric shock to my scalp. Strands of my wet hair had found their way into the socket of the light-bulb and across the terminals. For a dangerous second, I was lit up. Had Dr. Frankenstein been bending over me, I shouldn't have been surprised.

Probably saved from death by my thick-soled, rubber "daps" and the fact that fuses blew, somewhere along the corridor, I felt the thump of the current up and down and across the length, breadth and depth of my damp body, and then it was over. My hair was dry but people were roaming the corridor outside my room, trying to find the cause of the premature "Lights Out". I told no-one that I was, grateful for the luck that had kept me alive.

When the lights came back on, I was no nearer solving my problem and it was clear to me now, that, even using my torch and reading through "Lights Out", I wasn't going to get a grip of the whole of that text before morning. I'd read a few scenes from the beginning. I'd done the unforgivable and found out how it ended but I wasn't going to score many marks for skimpy knowledge such as that.

H. M. Dowling, our Pembroke Dock County Intermediate School headmaster, had taught us the importance of soliloquies. "They sum the character up", he'd said. "So, know your soliloquies." I fell back on his advice and, on what actors call, my "quick study". I fell asleep very long after "lights out" reciting, by rote:

> "I know you all and will awhile uphold the unyoked
> humour of your idleness.
> Yet, herein, do I imitate the sun, who doth permit the
> base contagious clouds
> To cover up his beauty from the earth, that, being
> wanted, he may be more wondered at."

By morning, I knew it all. I know it now.

I knew, too, of the King's admiration for Hotspur: "Thou makest me sad and makest me sin in envy that my Lord, Northumberland, should be the father to so blessed a son", and his disapproval of the apparent weaknesses of his own heir.

My second stroke of luck came that morning. When I opened the Literature paper in the Examination Hall, after breakfast, the first question read: "Show, from your knowledge of the text of Henry IV, Part One, the justification of Bradley's opinion that Shakespeare liked his villains more than his heroes." I was home and – as my shocked locks had been – dried. By such chances, reputations of academia can be made or lost.

Teaching literature to sixth-formers years later, I found, by accident, an amusing story about the enormous influence of Andrew Cecil Bradley, sometime professor of literature at Liverpool, at Glasgow and, at the turn of the century, professor of poetry at Oxford. The author of "Shakespearean Tragedy" and "Oxford lectures on poetry", he dominated Shakespearean scholarship until just about our time in Trinity. "Llew" Llewellyn was still under his spell when he tutored us, though we did know that people such as L. C. Knights were debunking him.

It seems that a candidate for scholarship entrance to the Civil Service faced a 'character' question, not on the text of a play but on Bradley's opinion of what Shakespeare was really saying in the play. Unable to cope, he turned to his own poetic talents. His examiner found the lad's verse instead of a well-versed Bradleyan answer on Shakespeare's verse.

> "I dreamed, last night, that Shakespeare's ghost
> Sat for this Civil Service post.
> The English papers of that year
> Were based on questions from King Lear
> Which Shakespeare answered very badly
> Because he hadn't studied Bradley."

I knew how the boy felt! I'd had better luck than he. I hope that they passed him and gave him the job.

Carmarthen, although almost a transit camp, surrounded as it was with hutted and tented military villages for the most part, seemed to escape the attention even of the casual, stray German bombers, which were in the habit of dumping their loads anywhere after aborted raids elsewhere. Tucked away in the narrows of the Tywi Valley, its people could hear the deep-throbbing enemy aircraft lining up their runs to blitz Swansea to the east and Pembroke Dock to the west, but it's difficult even to remember the air-raid sirens going at Trinity in 1943, 1944 and 1945. I notice, too, that the photograph of the Wing shows its window-panes already free of the criss-crossed masking-tape that, elsewhere in Britain, and certainly in Neyland, Pembroke Dock and Swansea, were mandatory protection from shattering glass.

The first flying bombs – the comically constructed but deadly "buzz bombs" and "doodle-bugs" – had taken Britain by surprise in the dark before dawn on the 13th June. 9,000 of them were launched across the Channel, although 25 per cent of them failed and fell – often turned, according to legend or propaganda or truth, by Hurricane fighter pilots taking them on, wingtip to wingtip – before crossing the English coast. They killed more than 6,000 people, seriously injured 18,000, causing savage destruction and concern, especially in London, before our advancing armies overran their continental launching sites, and Hitler was left with one more "Secret Weapon". Neither of them was aimed at West Wales.

During the summer holiday, as I walked through the bracken hand-in-hand with a quite different Glenys, there was a bomb-plot on Hitler's life; the Americans captured Guam; an uprising occurred in Warsaw; Allied forces landed in southern France; Marseilles was captured; Rumania surrendered; Paris was liberated; James Arthur "Jim" Davies was betrayed by a "double-agent" to the Nazis; and, on 3rd September, our second year at Trinity began.

For nearly six months, the just-out-of-his-teens Jim Davies had, with the enormous help of the Dutch "underground", successfully evaded capture. Now, new and frighteningly unpleasant experiences were about to begin for him. He was betrayed by a planted double-agent. In a German Orderly Room, in a Belgian prison, surrounded by German guards, he took on yet another identity. He was arraigned as a "spy and saboteur" under the prison number 698. Death seemed imminent. Thrown into "a filthy little cell", awaiting, as he thought, execution, he was fed ersatz coffee, turnip soup and "two slices of bread and fat" per day.

What he did not expect was to be shipped out to Germany by train but, on 26th August, 1944, he had left Brussels for Cologne. Now, re-classified again, as an R.A.F. flier, he and many others faced the wrath of survivors of the fire-storm in the ashes of Cologne Station, and might well have been killed there and then. He wasn't and, incredibly, was carried on – as the German European empire contracted – to Breslau in Poland. Boncath in Pembrokeshire might well have seemed for ever unattainable to him then.

On the 8th of September, a new German super-weapon, the "V-2", a sub-stratosphere rocket – quickly dubbed "the flying gas-pipe" – fell on Britain. Simultaneously, Allied forces fought their way into the German Fatherland. The parachute drop and glider-borne "glorious failure" of Arnheim almost coincided with the Asian First Battle of the Philippines. That other secret weapon potentially deadly – was grounded as its launching-sites were overrun but, in effect, the space-race had begun that would take men to the moon.

The Germans crushed the Warsaw uprising but the British landed in Greece and, with their allies, captured Athens. In December, as civil war broke out in the ancient Greek capital, German forces rallied and fought back in the Ardennes. It was to be their last counter-attack in the West. The Russians – rolling relentlessly forward, as the Allies raced them to political prizes – surrounded Budapest, the beautiful twin-city of the Danube.

Trinity College went down for Christmas; the last Christmas of the war. Peace and goodwill to all men weren't evident on earth. The wooden Church Hall at Neyland, though, caught some of the spirit of it as it bounced up and down to the jitter-bugging feet of the overcrowded "Welcome Home Fund" dances and the international and national couples; the men for the most part uniformed, and girls in their tank-tops, short skirts, bobby-socks and daps.

At home, and in chapel, we gathered – metaphorically, because Baptists didn't, then, go in for graven images – around the Crib. All the family other than Bryn, my soldier brother, were at home. We shared unexpected bounty with an advance party of Royal Engineers – half-a-dozen men or more whom Dad had invited to Christmas dinner from their bleak billets. Their Commanding Officer, on hearing of Dad's invitation to his men to join our family meal, sent a 15-cwt truck, piled with Christmas fare, around to our house. We were not having a bad war that week, though much of the world was bleeding to death.

After Christmas, we were back in College, when allied bombing took the "fire storm" to Dresden; ten days after, the Heads of State "summit" conference was held at Yalta.

The Americans went in to Okinawa; our troops and their allies captured Cologne; the Russians entered Vienna and – as he began to see victory on the horizon – President Roosevelt died of a massive brain haemorrhage. Two days later, the American and the Russian armies met and linked arms in Germany and – with Russian troops surrounding Berlin – Hitler shot his mistress, Eva Braun, before taking his own life in the underground bunker of the Chancellory gardens.

With a symmetry that almost seems to make a nonsense of coincidence, two days earlier, Il Duce, Benito Mussolini, the deposed idol of Fascist Italy, was saved the trouble of making such domestic arrangements. Italian partisans were the undertakers for that man and his mistress. Their bodies were strung from lamp-posts. Bertie Snow would have approved.

My father, as a Christian minister, presided over many funerals. He was a sharing, caring man – a comforter. He was a realist, too. "The cemeteries of the world", he used to quote, "are full of indispensable people."

Franklyn Roosevelt, the patrician democrat; Benito Mussolini, the fascist demagogue; Adolf Hitler, the national socialist despot;

were, all three, dispensed with, in five days, after dominating the warring world for five years. Thomas Gray had warned them.

> "The boast of heraldry, the pomp of power,
> And all that beauty, all that wealth e'er gave,
> Awaits alike th' inevitable hour:–
> The paths of glory lead but to the grave."

The paths of vain-glory, too, come to the same end, though Hitler's grave seems to have been a petrol-soaked pit and Mussolini hung – upside down and naked – high in the air, for ridiculing, before he found one.

And, all over Europe, men, women and children had died, in their millions, going to their unmarked graves, untimely, because politicians raise more echoes than poets and, as Thomas Gray hinted, people seem slower to follow a Cromwell "guiltless of his country's blood" than strutting demagogues who wave flags in their faces and give them Jack-boots for their feet.

Meanwhile, I'd been rusticated from Trinity. Yes! I had. No! I'd not been caught "in flagrante", but I had picked up a communicable infection.

During the Easter vacation, I'd taken a job. John Davies, the Co-op, the Bethesda Treasurer, was an Urban Councillor. Neyland Council was preparing to put in a sewerage system after the war, and a London firm of surveyors had been contracted to carry out extensive measurements of land-fall and out-fall and to prepare contracts. They needed two "chain-men", who knew the district, to act as general assistants and to hold the rods for theodolite measurements. Mr. Davies's grandson, Mervyn Averil, and I were employed.

The weather was fine. The work was agreeable. When my holiday drew to an end, there were still well-paid tasks to do, partly out on the Cleddau, in Bill Lloyd the ferry-man's boat, dropping floats with flags into the water at specified points and retrieving them. My father arranged a delayed return to College for me. During those extra sea-borne days, I became very badly sun-burned. So much so that I eventually returned to Trinity with a growth of beard over sore skin.

When it had healed enough to let me shave, I found that I'd left my safety razor at home. Stupidly, I borrowed one. Even more foolishly, I borrowed one with a blade that had already shaved its owner. The inevitable happened. I picked up this communicable disease, and the Coll. Doc. had to join his own queue for the attentions of Dr. Humphreys, who studied the rash briefly and wrote me a note to present at the Principal's office.

When Miss Francis read it, she blanched. "Impetigo?" she gasped. "Impetigo? You won't come too close, will you? Stand over there and wait a moment."

When she came back, she told me that the Principal had agreed to my going home again. "You must report to your own doctor this very day", she said. "I do hope that he can clear it up for you!" Shrinking from me, she slammed the half-window shut. What would she have done with a leper?

Sitting in the railway carriage as it ran past Westfield Mill and under Darky's Bridge, I felt that I should have a bell in one hand and a card saying "UNCLEAN" in the other. Treatment of impetigo wasn't the easiest thing to bear: nail-brushes, sulphur ointment and gentian violet featured in it in pre-penicillin days, but it passed, and I was glad to get back into College routine. "You should have used Lysol", said my father.

By now, not only were there a million captured German soldiers on mainland Europe; there was a camp full of them between Johnstown and the wooded escarpment at Ystrad. There was another camp, for German officers, at Bridgend. Some of these were high-ranking, and many of them were hard-line Nazis. There was truculence at Bridgend, as the war went sour on them. I seem to remember a hanging of a more liberal man, and think that the death was not suicide. Secretly, the German escape committee had been digging a tunnel. There came a day when a large number of them – more than 50 – used it and escaped.

Normally, our practice runs, as Harriers, took place on a Wednesday but, on that Tuesday afternoon, something went wrong with our handwork arrangements and we were left with free time. "Let's go for a run today, instead", someone suggested. "We can go to the matinée tomorrow, then."

It was a good idea on a lovely day. We kitted out and ran off. I don't remember who elected to pioneer a new route but we headed through Johnstown and took the road that would have us run past the prisoner-of-war camp. It was set well back from the road, of course, but, as we drew abreast of it, we could see a soccer game going on and prisoners standing around watching

Trinity and King Alfred's Colleges, Carmarthen – Harriers, 1944-45.

Back row, left to right: R. Eustis, D. P. Edwards, G. John, N. O. Davies, P. Robbins, M. N. Parfitt.

Front row: D. Oliver, W. G. Thomas (Vice-captain), G. Rees (Captain), J. A. Davis (Secretary), S. D. G. Parry.

N. O. Davies, third from right, rear row, is the brother of former student, J. A. Davies, who, at the moment that this photograph was taken was 'missing, presumed killed' but, in fact, 'walking back to Boncath through Nazi-occupied Europe'.

it. Nosey, as adolescents are, some of us jumped up on to the hedge to get a better look.

Crazy, as adolescents can be, we weren't quiet for long. At first, we were content to cheer the distant players derisively. "Keep it on the island!" "Watch him Ref!" That sort of thing. Then clowning began, and one or two – perhaps I was one of them? – began marching up and down on the road, stiff-kneed and heavy-footed, "goose-stepping", with our right arms raised, shouting, "Tonner und blitzen!" "Zeig heil!" "Raus! Raus! Raus!" and suitable phrases from "The Spy in Black" or the pages of "Beano". Before long, we were shouting "Heil Hitler!"

When the joke staled, we took off again on our innocent run. We hadn't gone far when we were overhauled by a British military truck. It passed us and rounded a bend ahead of us. A second vehicle was slowing down behind us. As we came, in our turn, to the bend, we found an officer and three soldiers standing in the road facing us. Their truck was on the grass verge.

"I'd like a word with you", the officer said. "Who are you? Where do you come from? What are you doing here?" The other vehicle had disgorged four more soldiers and they matched us one for one. What's more, they were all armed.

Not only had our pantomime been noticed by camp-guards but we'd chosen to do the German act when the Welsh countryside was being scoured for escaped prisoners-of-war. We were saved by our Welsh accents and our apologies, despite having added to their suspicions of us in answering a further question.

"How often do you go running like this?" asked the Captain. "Every Wednesday", said someone. "Why are you doing it on Tuesday, then?" he demanded. Then, they sent us on our way, but they must have double-checked with the College because Dai Griff reprimanded us for "silliness".

I did one more foolish thing that day. I wrote a suitably enhanced account of it home to my parents. "Interrogated" became "Arrested". The grass verge questioning was moved to "the gates of the camp". Instead of being hundreds of yards away from Germans, I talked of "eye-ball to eye-ball confrontation". I'd forgotten that Edgar Evans and Willie "Hot'un" Thomas – reporters for the "West Wales Guardian" and the "Western Telegraph and Cymric Times" – called at our house once a week for my father's chapel news. Dad read them my graphic account of my "clash with the military". They published it.

Cecil Parry's family sent him the local papers weekly, as did mine to me. "What's all this, then?" he asked, knowing the actual story. "Polished it up a bit, haven't you?" I had, indeed, until it was a shining example of how not to burnish a tale that is good enough in itself; not if you're writing to proud parents, anyway! Incidentally, all of those escaped prisoners-of-war were recaptured eventually. I believe that some of them were in shorts and vests and daps.

We hadn't much longer to go at Trinity. I hadn't been conscious of time speeding or dragging, but our Final exams concentrated our minds for a week or so, after Easter, and we had the spectacular excitement, in the first week of May, of the announcement of the end of the war against Germany.

Between morning and evening of Monday, 7th May, we'd realised that the German war was over. Soon, we would learn that – at one minute past midnight on 8th May – the Victory in Europe would be marked with a national day of celebration; the first V.E. Day. For almost a third of our lives, my generation had listened to news of war. Now, with news of peace, we stood together on the College steps in the late afternoon.

No-one had told us to gather there but we did. More remarkably, so did the staff. Principal Halliwell and his staff stalwarts – Captain Ithel Thomas; H. L. Harby; John Humphreys; David Griffiths: "Llew" Llewellyn; Stanley Moss and, even Miss Francis – were all caught up in the excitement that was running wild-fire throughout the whole of Britain.

There was a flag-pole on a cupola on the roof of the then college library. Someone, probably the old soldier, suggested that the Union flag should be flying from the naked pole. In those days, before the Red Dragon was officially flown, and the Board of Education had only just become a Ministry, the Union Jack still seemed appropriate, even at Trinity.

There was a problem of logistics and access, but there was no trouble in finding the Union Jack. It appeared among us on the steps. The problem was that there was no cord through the pulley of the flag-pole, and the rope that should have been there was attached to the flag.

"How", asked the Principal, "can we get it up there?"

My moment of victory glory had come.

Growing up, as I had, in John Street, Neyland, I had served an apprenticeship in running the roofs of educational buildings. The John Street gang, had, at one time, scaled the peaks of their primary school at night, in secret triumph over the teachers who taught them under those roofs by day. Shinning up a drainpipe was second nature to us. We had found tight-roof running easier than slack-wire walking.

In any case, the library roof was only head and shoulders above us, and it was the matter of a second to volunteer, seize the flag, mount the shoulders of a mate, and haul myself into the little valley of the roof. Student noises egged me on – always more derisory than supportive – more ironic than admiring. They were a stimulation, nonetheless. My shoes were rubber-soled and heeled, leather having gone off the market during the war, and I was equipped for showing off.

Pulling myself upright, I walked the peak of the roof, hearing the encouraging voices of Roy Eynon, Tod Davies, Teddy Bevan, Gordon John and Charlie Evans out of my Neyland childhood, rather than those of my colleagues of the College. "You can do it, Gord", they were saying. "Don't look down, look up." "Don't slow down, keep going."

I knew that I could do it. With an audience that big and that important, there was no way that I was going to fall. I was on the cupola in seconds. It took minutes to thread the pulley and rather less to hoist the flag and make the painter fast. The return journey was even easier. It was a matter of sliding to the shoot, climbing down the pipe, and I was grounded again.

Perhaps I am the only one who remembers that small involvement of mine in Trinity's salute to victory. We were invited immediately afterwards to follow the Principal to the College Chapel, where a Service of Thanks would be offered.

Robed and ready, now, for that other part of his life, as an Anglican Priest, the Principal ushered us in to worship. There was more excitement in the air than the splendid College Chapel usually expected. There was a better timbre to the hand-pumped organ music. There was a rising cadence in the singing of the first hymn. The calling and responding went well, and it was only then that Principal Halliwell made his mistake.

Before going into the pulpit with his appropriate sermon of satisfaction that the war was over, he made a domestic announcement from the chancel steps.

"There are going to be some days of public holiday to celebrate V.E. Day", he told us. "So, as soon as this service is over, you may leave for your homes." Before his back was turned for him to face the pulpit steps, that good man's congregation was diminishing fast. Forty-year-old ex-soldiers led the retreat; some of them using combat techniques to keep out-of-sight behind the pews, as platoons of them headed for the side of the organ, and escaped into the ante-chapel. By the time the little sermon was over, only more-or-less local students were left. The others were already racing for the railway station or queuing for the bus in Lammas Street.

I remember my own journey home on a very early train out of Carmarthen the next morning. There was very little hitch-hiking, as I've said. You know that petrol was rationed, traffic was mostly military. Young men in civilian clothes were slightly suspect, and soldiers already in service either ignored them or questioned when they were going to "get some time in?" The train was packed, 1st, 2nd and 3rd Class ticket-holders stood, with their baggage – civilian or military – one nation for once.

Neyland, as you know, had become a service centre as the war peaked. Army, Air Force, Navy and, by then, Wrens, A.T.S. and W.A.A.F.s. were billeted in and around the town and at Pembroke Dock. Uniforms were everywhere. My father, arm-banded "O.C.F.", was an officiating Chaplain to the Forces. Everyone had something to celebrate, and it seemed to be Christmas Day, Easter holiday, Bank Holiday Monday and Scoveston Fort Races rolled into one. My friends were in the streets. The European war really was over now. Peace had broken out. We were about to make maximum use of it in our own interests.

Although it would be three years before he became my father-in-law, Jack Incledon came up with the idea. A formidable drummer on a good evening, whose repertoire began and ended with "In 11 more months and 12 more days, I'll be out of the calaboose!", he suggested that we form a sort of skiffle-band and set off around the streets of the town. Apart from the big drum, skinned on one side by a piece of barrage balloon, since velum was unobtainable, instruments were hard to come by. There was a clapped-out bugle, and someone who could blow the scale on it. There was a mandolin, lacking much of a musician. There was a guitar. Last in the queue, and lacking musicianship, I was handed the horn of a dead gramophone, out of which I produced some tuneless but interesting noises, more or less rhythmically. Billy Cotton would have been surprised, to say the least, given the sophistication that has since developed in such things. People would probably be impressed even now, to see such a Rag, Tag, and Bobtail band take to the streets, but take to them we did, gathering strength as we went. We had not gone far before we had attracted more children to our train than the Pied Piper of Hamelin, or Charlie Wilford!

The chapels and the pulpits were empty that evening, but the pubs were full, and our progress up the High Street into Kensington Road, down the long slope to Water Street, and up the incline to Honeyborough, was punctuated by the pleasure that our arrival gave to the celebrations at the New Inn, The Coburg, The Forresters, The Commercial and The Oddfellows Inn. It was at one of the hostelries that someone threw money into my enamelled trumpet. Before long, the noises coming out of it were muted by the money pouring into it, and later, along the road, I had to call in assistance to help to shoulder it, as half-crowns, florins, bobs and tanners, old pennies, half-pennies and farthings tumbled into it. Our celebratory band became a collecting group for the Neyland "Welcome Home Fund". It was just as well, because what little music there had been had become staccato as the "musicians" became breathless, and some, legless. The few of us who were still teetotallers had to form in phalanx to hold the group together.

When we returned to 39 High Street and emptied "His Master's Voice" on to the kitchen table, we had collected £38.16s.3d., or it might have been £33.18s.6d. Whatever it was, it was enough in those days to warrant a later letter from Councillor J. C. G. John, the Chairman of the Welcome Home Fund Committee, to my future father-in-law, thanking him for his public spirit. My mother-in-law-to-be kept the letter until her dying day, long after his, and it is probably among the family papers now.

Councillor J. C. G. John, by the way, was a nephew of two of the earliest of the students at the South Wales and Monmouthshire College, and his son, Michael and Michael's daughter, Penny, succeeded him at Trinity.

The public spirit, though, was still running freely – or, rather, reasonably cheaply – in the public-houses of the town. Private bottles, saved for the great occasion, were being uncorked, and Neyland celebrations were rising to a climax.

Before dark, we lifted Mrs. Margaret Perkins' piano out of the sitting-room of her house in High Street on to the pavement in front of Llewellyn's Cash Exchange. The flat-roof of the air-raid shelter under the police station bank, levelling on to the grass, was thronged with people. No-one sent out any notices, but the drum had only just been set up alongside the piano, and the strolling players reconstituted, when the audience gathered. They came from everywhere. A true pianist had been found in a local lady. Wallace Lewis, lately a "Desert Rat", had been one of our band. He played a string on a broom-handle set in half a tea-chest. Whatever part he'd played in his long and foreign service, he was home and happy, and tireless in the celebration of peace. Rhythms were steadier. Throats – well oiled and lubricated – were in good voice, and the finest impromptu concert of Neyland's history began. Its programme was to last into the night and towards the morning.

As we sang the patriotic songs of Empire, we rolled out the barrel – musically and literally – 'hung out' our washing on the Siegfried line' and generally jazzed up our relief. Wasn't the War to end all Wars over?

CHAPTER TWELVE

The Conclusions

Well! No! It wasn't, was it? The war to end all wars wasn't over. A phase of it was, temporarily. One major theatre-of-war had exchanged hands. Victors had become vanquished. Nations that had been over-run by the Nazis were run over again by their conquerors. Countries that had been made satellites of the Third Reich became puppets of other systems, communist imperialism taking "the eastern bloc" and democratic triumphalism securing the "free west" of Europe. Germany was divided, Berlin was subdivided. The alliances of the hot war were over. The "Cold War" had already begun.

Perhaps, after the first flush of relief at the removal of the devil that you'd come to know, there wouldn't – for a long time afterwards – have seemed to have been much difference, much lightening of the heavy hand and foot of total government. Initially, the liberators would have had to be totalitarian, too, and if you were living in the cellars under the rubble of your home, or traipsing someone else's countryside, trying to get back to your own, you might wonder, occasionally, what had happened to your dreams.

Hunger is hunger. Grief is grief. Cold is cold. A curfew is a curfew, whatever uniform polices it. Freedom is food, clothing and shelter. It's going where you want to go, with whomsoever you choose, whenever you choose. It's thinking what it pleases you to think and saying whatever you have to say. It's fearing no foot in your door, or your face, by day or night. It's having no man's hand on your collar. And organising that for the devastated Europe would consume generations yet.

Anyway, there was, still, escalating war in Asia, where "the forgotten armies" were waging it by night and day.

Just then, too, the discovery of the ghastly concentration camps caught the emotions of the world by the throat as the skeletal survivors of the viciousness of man's inhumanity to man benefited immediately from being freed, doctored, fed, clothed and comforted. They had survived Hell on earth. They were alive, just. But millions were not. Their racked and rigoured corpses lay in the lime-pits.

After the euphoria of our celebrations of V.E. Day had died away, we'd reassembled in Trinity for the conclusions of our times there. It simply wouldn't have been adequate to write "the conclusion of our time there". The singular couldn't cover all that was coming to an end that early summer.

Tuesday, the 8th of May – with the "one minute past midnight" marking of the End of World War II against Germany – was only the first of many conclusions.

Naturally, I recalled my father's grave voice telling his congregation more than five years earlier: "My dear friends, for the second time in the lives of many of us, we are at war with Germany."

Where one British Prime Minister, Neville Chamberlain, had raised – perhaps only in his own mind – hopes of "peace in our times", another, Churchill, Winston Spencer, had challenged the nation to be sceptical, even in victory, on the long road to a sort of peace. The great phrase-maker – in a speech at The Mansion House, London, on the 10th of November, 1940, in reference to victories in the battle for Egypt – had set things in context.

"This is not the end. It is not even the beginning of the end. But it is, perhaps, the end of the beginning."

That's how it was for us – as, indeed, it was for the world – while the little life-time of our two years in Trinity ran towards its conclusions.

But how was it for Jim Davies? You'll scarcely believe this! As though all the travels and travails of the months "underground" had not been enough – rounded off as they had been in a castle prisoner-of-war camp in Upper Silesia, where, in the finest traditions of the "Welsh in dispersion", he'd formed a Welsh society, a concert party, and a choir – he was, now, incarcerated in a "bloody awful place" at Luckenwalde, forty miles from Berlin.

Walking on ill-shod feet again, in a column of 6,000 British, American, Russian and French prisoners-of-war, he had lived through the infamous "march of despair" that the now-panicking Nazi leaders had imposed – in the face of the rampaging advances of the Red Army of Russia – on the occupants of their prisoner-of-war camps in East Germany and Poland. All of them had been herded along 300 miles of bombed-out roads, country lanes and snow-covered fields, trudging, stumbling through mud, ice and misery, wracked with dysentery and debilitation, starving, vomiting, gangrenous from frost-bite; all driven to the point of death – and many, beyond it. Some survived as many as 500 miles on that march of misery, through the frozen, hell-on-earth of shattered Germany. Most, in the process, lost more than a third of their body-weight. Many lost limbs – maimed beyond repair – amputated at the roadside.

Naturally, along the way, Jim had escaped. It was not a classic, over-or-under-the-wire break-out. He'd just turned down a side-street, out of the ghastly, funeral parade and tapped on a front-door of a terraced house. A German hous-frau had helped him from her door-step in to her kitchen and given him "a bucket of soup" which he'd "drained" before there was a second knocking on that door.

A German guard had watched Jim disappear and had come to take him back to the shuffle of despair. He was to take him back, too, to the early idiocies of the Cold War, as the survivors of the march became pawns in the check and counter-check of human chess played out in the ruins of Western Europe.

In a frustrating finalé to his astonishing war-time walkabout, James Arthur Davies became, for a while, a prisoner of the Russian conquerors of East Berlin. The cosy communism of the Capitol Cinema, Carmarthen, was a total contrast with the frozen-solid and grim attitudes that emerged as allies faced-down erstwhile allies in the struggle for power over anarchic events.

There were to be another six weeks of unnecessary, protracted suffering – of queuing for potato-peelings thrown out of camp-kitchen doors – before, far into malnutrition and ounces from starvation, he was freed and, finally, on his way home to the Preselis. His walking back to Boncath was over. He was travelling "on the cushions" now.

Within days, this former Trinity College student, this future Trinity College lecturer, was to arrive at Carmarthen Station. Hear him tell it.

"There was an emotional reception two days later when I arrived home. The entire village turned out for the official welcome to the only member of that closely-knit community who had once been declared 'Missing, presumed killed', and who had returned. My parents and my brother, Nefydd, were in the hired car which was driven by Griff-y-Bys from Carmarthen station to our local village. It was towed in for the last few hundred yards by my former school friends." There is a foot-note. "I was now under six-stone in weight and suffered from muscular rheumatism." But our boy was back in Boncath, and he would soon be into all sorts of good works in Pembroke-shire.

Jim's brother, Nefydd, incidentally, hadn't far to go to rendez-vous with his returning hero. Davies, N. O., Bryn Hedydd, Bon-cath, Pembrokeshire, had a room in the Wing. He had been a junior contemporary of ours and a Harrier alongside me since September, 1944. When, as a youngester, he had heard that his idolised older brother was missing and presumed dead, he'd told his grieving parents that he would do the things that Jim had hoped to do. His entry to Trinity was his first step along that way. Later, Nefydd became a distinguished head-teacher of Llandudno's school for children with special needs.

Given all the other coincidences and caffled lifelines in this tangled tale of mine, does it surprise you that the equally admired head-teacher who succeeded Nefydd Davies, when he moved on to other things, was T. M. Rhapps: he of the soft-soled organ boots?

While the Naval air attacks on Japan escalated at the end of May, we sat our Final Examinations and worried about how well or how badly we might have done. That sounds silly in the context of holocaust. The priority seemed reasonable to us at the time. We do live where we are.

At that time, too, a conference of western world leaders was convened in San Francisco, California, in the U.S.A. It might just still prove to have been the most important meeting to have been held anywhere in the world in my long lifetime. Or, then, again, it might not.

We don't know for certain yet. It's only been half-a-century since that meeting. Heads of state and their advisers talked and talked in San Francisco. Churchill had a sentence for that, too.

Much later, on the 26th of June, 1954, in Washington, he said: "To Jaw-jaw is better than to war-war."

He said that because, on the 26th of June, 1945, at that San Francisco Conference, the United Nations Charter had been signed. As a result, the United Nations Organisation had been set up. A nascent Parliament of the World had, in the decade since, talked and talked, voted and vetoed, created agencies and organisations, to intervene at points of crisis in human affairs and to promote and establish security, justice, welfare and human rights world-wide, for all people.

If the Charter were to be observed, in letter and spirit, by the 51 states that signed up to it in 1945, or, better still, by the 113 nations that had done so by 1965, the member-countries would achieve a safer, saner world, it was thought. Fifty years later, the world is waiting.

As signatories, they had agreed to and accepted four main duties. They would settle all disputes peacefully. They would refrain from threatening or using force. They would assist in implementing the Charter. They would not assist or co-operate with an aggressor nation. Finally, they affirmed faith in the human rights of all human beings without distinction of race, sex or religious faith.

These conclusions from San Francisco, coinciding with our coming to ours in Carmarthen, seemed to mean that we would be going out to work and live in an optimistic, trouble-free world.

Charlie Wilf made the point to us one morning. He was clearly miffed. “Do you know how lucky you are?” he asked, quite unashamedly envious. “You will shortly be going down”, he said, “for the longest vacation of your lives.”

At that time, once the Final Examinations were over, and other commitments – to courses, to college societies and sporting fixtures – discharged, we were allowed to go home before term had officially ended. Since schools normally re-opened on the 1st September, we could, effectively, have part of June and the whole of July and August on holiday. A pleasant prospect for us, it was mildly irritating to our master of music.

“Make the most of it”, he warned. “Don’t let it go to your head. Teaching is hard work. You’ve got to like it, you know. You’ve got to like teaching. You’ve got to like kids. It’s no good thinking of being a teacher because of long holidays.

“I tell you, gentlemen, I pity the man who goes into teaching and doesn’t like kids. They know, you know, kids. They’ll find your weaknesses and they’ll break you.

“If you’re a born teacher, it’ll be different. If you give them your best, you might bring the best out of them. That’s a good feeling, that. It’s what keeps us going in the classroom. What else would have kept us going on what used to be called a salary on the pre-Burnham Scale. We worked for a pittance."

Charlie was smarting a bit, too, because, assuming we were to find teaching posts, we would be entering the classrooms as the highest-paid probationer teachers ever to pick up chalk in the public education system of Britain.

H. L. Harby hadn't missed this point either. The Butler Education Act, now on the statute book, had created new scales of pay for teachers that, for a while, were much better than those of college lecturers.

"I cannot believe, gentlemen", Harby had said when the new Burnham agreement was announced, "I cannot believe that there is anyone in this craft workshop this morning – other than me – who is worth £320 for his first year in the classroom. What's more, I cannot believe that anyone here will ever be worth £650 a year, other than me."

He said it, of course, with a wry grin. He was pulling our legs. There was, though, a touch of pain and a heavy weight of incredulity behind his teasing.

My father was incredulous, too; pleased for me, but surprised. "It's a good job, teaching", he said, later. "Good, clean work. Good, clean conditions. And a pension at 65!"

Having spread muck and cleared out cow-sheds; as a lad, cut coal and quarried slate, as a man, before getting his "good, clean job" in the pulpit – satisfying a calling, a vocation, into the bargain – he appreciated the advantages of the career now open to his youngest child. A few months later, we compared his pastor's monthly cheque with my first one as a teacher.

Mine was for £26. Dad's was for £23. I had served my first full month in the classroom. Fifty-two-years-old, he was in his twenty-second year as a Christian minister and had spent almost as many before that as a farm-boy, a quarry-man and a coal-miner. As to the pension at 65, I was not too excited. I was 19-years-old at the time.

That comparison of salaries was to come later. Let's go back for a moment to the month of May, 1945. Let's remember, too, the long-ago interviews that Cecil Parry and I had had at Pembrokeshire's County Education Offices in Haverfordwest. You'll recall that we had both filled in forms of application for teaching posts in our home county. To be honest, I'd almost forgotten that myself at that time.

With the war ending, I'd been giving more thought to teaching service overseas. National Service couldn't be far away. Some people were talking about the military schools being set up in Europe. The Baptist Missionary Society's own need for teachers in foreign lands came back to mind.

Then, one day, I received a telegram. Telegrams were a delight. They were, also, a wartime distress. They were replaced too early by the clumsy Express Letter that implied neither the fun nor the urgency of receiving "a wire". The Fax, later, and now "E"-mail and the Internet, have made the telegram, "the wire", obsolete. The yellow-enveloped "Immediate Delivery" message, typed on strips stuck on to an off-white, G.P.O. pro-forma, came to my hand as I was in the North Hall, checking whether there was any conventional mail for me.

My first thoughts were for my father. He had begun to faint and fall about and give my mother reason to be concerned for him. Was he the cause of my telegram? In the long run, he probably had been, but there was nothing about him in it.

Addressed "Gordon Parry, Student, Trinity College, Carmarthen", it was from Mr. D. T. Jones, M.A., Director of Education for the County of Pembroke. It read: "Noting that you have studied Advanced Handicraft during your college course, I propose to appoint you to the staff of The Coronation School, Pembroke Dock. Please contact my office. D. T. Jones".

Nepotism must have been at work. D. T. Jones and T. L. Parry were good friends. Mr. Jones's deputy, Tim Davies, was a Baptist deacon and Chapel secretary in Haverfordwest. Harold Thomas was, as you know, my Cadet Force Commanding Officer and Clerk to the Education Committee which Dad chaired. Ivor Thomas, from Neyland, knew me, too. I must have been running on an inside track.

Since the Coronation School needed a woodwork master, and I, with luck, was about to qualify to teach it, I was nominated by my father's friends. I was delighted. I didn't give "undue influence" a thought. "Where God guideth, He provideth" was closer to mind.

My Pembrokeshire coterie was good about it, too. No-one said: "It isn't what you know, it's who you know": not to me anyway. Eventually, all of us were to teach – Cecil Parry only for a while – in Pembrokeshire. Eric Orsman and Barry Owen both worked until they retired there – on pension, long before they were 65 – and immensely well-respected by their colleagues. My early appointment, to home, meant two things. One, my holiday was to be cut down. Two, our pleasant "gang" of friends was to break up early. I only discovered that when I telephoned the Pembrokeshire Education Office. There was one further reason for me to put thoughts of "abroad" out of my head: "going foreign" would have to be postponed.

Almost by the same delivery as the job-offer telegram, I had received a letter from my mother. She was increasingly worried about my father's health. He'd fallen on a slippery surface during the previous winter and the violent blow to his head had left him unconscious for minutes and dazed, disorientated, amnesiac for hours. Since then, he had suffered these convulsive, fainting episodes. He called them "attacks". In fact, they were fits. Diagnosed later as petit mal, controlled and, ultimately cleared, they were that summer occurring with increasing frequency. My mother's letter was a "Come home and help us" plea. It ended: "There is so much that you could do in the Sunday School, in the Band of Hope, in the Young People's Guild, to help your Dad but don't mention it when you write. Don't tell him I've asked, will you, Boy? He doesn't like to think that there's anything the matter with him, does he?"

In any case, I hadn't been about to turn down a job at the Coronation School. It had a famous history as "The Dockyard School". The Royal Admiralty Dockyard at Pembroke Dock had been known throughout the British Empire, during the full extent of its "glory", when imperialism was not a dirty word.

Some of the most dedicated teaching in Wales had contributed to an "Honours Board" – still proudly on display in the town – of scholars in mathematics, physics, practical sciences, and of Senior Constructors with the Admiralty who had been educated at "the Cora".

When the Dockyard had been closed in the 'twenties, the trauma had taken the economic heart out of the Pembroke peninsula. It had, inevitably, taken away the dynamic of that fine Admiralty-focused school. How badly it had been affected by the time I joined its staff will be another story.

Interestingly, in the context of this one, there had been a bonus for the South Wales and Monmouthshire Training College at Carmarthen. The soon-to-be Trinity College had recruited a brilliant group of students whose ambitions to become Admiralty men had been frustrated when their Dockyard School scholarship and practical apprenticeships no longer led to guaranteed service with the Crown. They had turned to teaching instead.

The College intake for 1929-1931 had more than a usual quota of Cleddau estuary men. I've counted a dozen names in the College's Year Book and Directory for that period. Most of those named were heading the teaching profession in Pembrokeshire when I went down from Trinity. They proudly sported their tricolour Trinity ties still.

There is no doubt that their swelling of the College register resulted, in the main, from the closure of the Pembroke Dockyard and, almost without exception, they were some of the finest teachers in my county, deserving of an Honours Board of their own.

Sam Bermingham was a classic example of the cadre. I knew him rather better than I might have done because he lived with his parents almost next-door to Flossie Griffiths's shop in Kensington Road, around the corner from our Manse. His mother was a cart-customer of mine and a first call on Saturday mornings. She ran, in their front room, an Old Curiosity Shop, charging a halfpenny to those who wished to see the ephemera laid out there.

The Berminghams were from travelling tinker stock. The memorabilia of their people's voyaging at home and abroad fascinated us. Their son, a brilliant mathematician, had been forced out of his apprenticeship and went, instead, via the burgeoning Trinity, to be a leader of his alternative profession; a distinguished teacher, head teacher, teacher-union official and local councillor.

I took my telegram up what seemed to me, then, the imposing staircase to the "Pearly Gates", the hole in the wall that was Principal Halliwell's last redoubt against student intrusion. I knocked, deferentially, on the fluted glass of one half of the famous sliding window. Miss Francis slid back the other half.

When she saw who was there, she almost shut it again. Alarm! "Impetigo!" signalled itself in the green, to amber, to red of her eyes: "My God! What has he caught now?" I think that both of us, for a moment, heard the leper-bell and the shout: "Unclean!" Framed in her hatch, her body concealed, she made a reverse "Leper squint" before she beat down her panic.

"Mr. Parry", she said, royally, "what may we do for you today?"

"Is it possible … Miss Francis …" I asked … "Is it possible for me to see Principal Halliwell?"

There was a fleeting return of doubt to her eyes. She was probably wondering if she could have me certified "F.F.I. – Free From Infection" before she negotiated an interview for me with the Supreme Being.

"Well, there's one thing about Impetigo", I thought. "It gets you noticed."

"May we ask, Mr. Parry", questioned la grande dame, "what it is that you wish to see the Principal about?"

"It's about this telegram, Miss Francis", I answered – growing a little in confidence and importance "I've had this telegram." To show how important I was becoming, I waved my yellow envelope.

"A telegram! Oh dear! I do hope that it's not bad news, Mr. Parry", the lady said in her longest-suffering voice.

Clearly, since my first appearance at her window, I had for ever, in her high mind, been associated with bad news. I did my best to ingratiate.

"No! It's good news, actually, Miss Francis", I said. "I've been offered a post."

I had chosen the ultimate word with care. To talk of teaching as "a job" to Miss Francis would have been as offensive as to call King George my uncle. Nevertheless, she still issued a pedantry – a small correction – patiently.

"A position, Mr. Parry", she corrected. "You've been offered a position. Well done! I'm sure the Principal will want to know about it."

Miss Francis clearly thought that "a post" was something that street dogs cocked up their legs against and she cocked up her nose at my choice of noun. I thought that "a position" was open to at least as much misinterpretation as a post but smiled back at her. A native-born peasant always shows respect to a butler, a sergeant major, and a secretary. Between them, they rule the world. Miss Francis was – as was the Trinity that she served – all three in one.

Principal Halliwell was kindness itself. I had been, finally, ushered into The Presence. As is almost always the case, the doorstep had been the last difficulty. Busy men don't necessarily build barriers around themselves but someone has to control access to them and to their time.

He was relaxed and welcoming. "It seems congratulations are in order", he said. "Do show me your telegram."

I handed it to him, still in its envelope. He read the addressing on the envelope and said, "Thank you, Gordon." It sounded strange to me, that! I'd become used to being "Sam". Even that Trinity identity of mine was coming to a conclusion. But, I realised that our Principal was a family man; a fatherly man. He asked about Dad.

"I know your father", the Rev. Mr. Halliwell said. "It seems that he's been unwell. I do hope that you'll find him better." Then: "A splendid school, The Coronation", he added. "This College has had friendly associations with it. We're still in touch with some of its ex-pupils who became students of ours. We shall probably see a number of them when we celebrate our Centenary in 1948. We're making plans for that already."

This was not, in fact, the first time that I'd been welcomed to the Principal's light and pleasant office. It was the second. As a member of a small group of students involved in organising the College "Rag" – its cheerful, charity carnival, when the gown went to town in circus style – I'd sat there before. I'd even taken part in the discussions. This day, though, I was there in my own right for the first and the last time. Nor was I there for long.

"You must telephone the Director. He'll be expecting to hear from you today. Miss Francis will let you 'phone from her office, I'm sure. Then, when you know a little more about your appointment, we shall see what needs to be done."

Back in the care of Miss Francis, I made the call. I asked to speak not to the Director, nor to Colonel, "Skipper", Harold Thomas, A.C.F. and Scouts, but to Mr. Ivor Thomas. He had my instructions ready for me. "We want you to begin as soon as possible", he said. "They'll be expecting you at "The Cora" at the end of this month." It was to be an abrupt conclusion to my college life.

As that man, Churchill, said, it was not the end. It was not even the beginning of the end. But it was, perhaps, the end of the beginning of my preparations for the classroom, and for thirty years and more, from the 1st July, 1945, I would go on learning to be a teacher. I would carry, too, throughout that time, a bonus of one quarter of a year of teaching service because I had taught for one month before the summer holidays of 1945. I was blessed, too, with pay for the month of August.

But we can't leave Trinity, just like that, can we? July, 1945, was too full of conclusions to be left simply with the small beginning of one man's career in the Coronation School, Pembroke Dock.

On the 5th of July, the Allies recognised Poland's new government. The Russians were consolidating the extended borders of their empire, and the western powers were simply turning "de facto" into "de jure".

In Britain, most of the month was devoted to the first General Election since 1935. The conventional wisdom about it was that the popular influence of Winston Churchill, "the man who won the war", would ensure that the Coalition wartime government would be replaced by a Conservative one. It wasn't. Churchill's deputy, Labour's under-estimated Clement Attlee, went to Downing Street, after a "landslide" victory won by his Party, on 26th of July. I heard the news of that astonishing – and, for me, delightful – conclusion, in the Coronation School's Lower Hall, relayed by word of mouth from the school's only wireless, in the Board Room, by staff who were as excited as I was. Ten years and a World War without electing a government gave us more interest in our masters than current voters can imagine.

Six days later, on 6th August, 1945, the first atomic bomb to be used in war in the history of the world dropped on Japan: "a missile", *The New York Times* said, on Tuesday, 7th August, "equal to 20,000 of T.N.T." Harry Truman, he of "If you can't stand the heat get out of the kitchen!" and "The buck stops here", warned the Japanese to prepare for a "Rain of ruin".

"By God's Mercy, British and American science outpaced all German efforts", said Prime Minister Churchill in a statement written before he left office. God's mercy would not have seemed too obvious that day in Hiroshima.

Ironically, Churchill's statement was issued to the media of the world – as *The New York Times* reported – "from 10 Downing Street by his successor, Clement R. Attlee."

On the 9th August, the paper's headlines read: "SOVIET DECLARES WAR ON JAPAN; ATTACKS MANCHURIA, TOKYO SAYS;" and, then, "ATOM BOMB LOOSED ON NAGASAKI." The "Rain of ruin" hadn't yet ended, nor would ruin cease to rain down there and elsewhere for a long time to come, but no-one knew about "nuclear fallout" that morning.

Then, on August 15th, 1945, just two weeks into the foreshortened "longest vacation of your lives" that Mr. Wilford had promised me, came the most sought-after, and, in terms of human life, the most expensive, conclusion of all. *The New York Times* bannered it.

"JAPAN SURRENDERS, END OF WAR".

Under the headline was a picture of the haberdasher President of the United States, Harry S. (The S standing for nothing) Truman, reading, to a group in the Oval Office of the White House, the text of the note from the Japanese government "accepting the terms of the Potsdam Declaration of July 26th, 1945, which amplified the Cairo Declaration of 1943". Japan ordered its people to "end hostilities". A "Cease-fire Order" was "Given to the Allied Forces".

And there it was! All that dying between 1943 and 1945, had coincided, day-to-day, with all our living at Trinity College, Carmarthen. We had been a part of it. We had been apart from it. Inevitably, the rest of our living until our dying, too, would be shaped by it.

As I'd left the upper corridors of power then, six momentous weeks were about to change the world. I had things still to do at Trinity College before I went home. Most of them were mundane; so much so that I don't remember doing them.

I do remember, though, that it was not only a time for farewells to friends. It was also a time for balancing books. The Minor Canon of Winchester Cathedral and Principal of King Alfred's College was, literally, in for a rude awakening. His little despotisms had been recorded. Scores had been kept. There were those who had resented leaving their warm beds unreasonably early to make sure that he was awakened for early communion, that his kettle was already boiling for his morning tea, and that he was roused precisely to the minute of his choice.

There were those – Choral Secretaries and such – who had suffered verbal abuse for arriving in his rooms too early; others for being late.

Alone among resident members of staff, the Rev. R. C. White organised a rota of batmen for himself. Perhaps he had done so in envy of his wife.

Yes! That had been a surprise! One day, a flagged and chevroned, camouflaged, military car, driven by an A.T.S. girl, had turned into the College grounds. Seated in the rear of it was an impressively high-ranking A.T.S. officer. I don't remember now whether her rank equalled that of a full colonel or of a brigadier. The most startling thing about that well-turned, well-turned-out and gallant lady was that she was married to Prinny White! By all accounts, she was as pleasant as she was important. I don't know. I never met the lady.

I do know, though, the whole story of the darkest-hour-before-dawn, rude awakening of her civilian husband from his slumbers. No doubt – intelligent as you are – you will remember that E. Barry Owen owned a cornet, a three-valved brass instrument of the trumpet family, and that he had it with him in College.

It's sufficient for you to know, too, that, with only a little while to go before they were to cease to be students, someone asked to borrow Barry's cornet.

Since summer nights are short, and darkness was necessary for cover, the person or persons – who must forever remain unknown – scarcely went to bed at all one night.

When it was, at last, dark enough, they – or was it he? – made their – or was it his? – silent way out of the Wing, down the steep, internal staircase, through the long corridor of the South Hall, off the Cloisters and up the stone stairways to the bachelor apartment where some had gathered almost two years earlier for the seminar on sex education. Tempted sorely, no-one giggled. A door was unlatched and opened soundlessly. Without any sound, either, the erstwhile lecture-room was checked. Black-out curtains, mandatory, even in summer-time, deepened the heavy dark. There was one more door to go. It was well-oiled, too, swinging back without whimpering.

In the deepest of the darkness, there was a four-poster bed. From that bed came the guiding sounds of stertorious breathing. The carrier of the cornet moved in. He filled his own lungs. He leaned forward, towards the pillowed head. Then he fingered the triple keys and licked his lips. Soon he would use his "triple tongue". A catch in breathing of the sleeper gave a split-second of absolute silence before the crescendos of "Colonel Bogey" beat back the dawn.

It was a simple message and "all that the band could play". It froze the frightened choirmaster to his cot just long enough for a repetition of the opening bars and a discordant snatch of a tenor voice singing a line that ended "and the same to you!" before doors were slammed on exit and a borrowed key turned in the last of them. Racing tennis daps slurped down the stairs and across the corridors. Reveille was over. Another small war had concluded in victory.

For the record, I must remind you that my mastery of the cornet ended at three bars of "Sweet Rosey O'Grady", and – tenor or not – I couldn't hold a tune. Not guilty. Quod erat demonstrandum.

No-one ever admitted to playing that dawn-of-day fanfare. No-one ever guessed who sang the solo. In fairness to the man who had been trumped and trumpeted, no-one was witch-hunted either. Perhaps Mr. White had been only too relieved to know that Gabriel hadn't been using the cornet, calling him home. As for Sam Parry, home was calling him.

When the train clickety-clacked, clickety-clacked, clickety-clacked, on its way to, through and beyond, Johnston, I crossed and criss-crossed the railway carriage again. In early summer, the valley was as green as Richard Llewellyn's ever was and I looked out on the leafy stream where I'd caught minnows and tickled small trout.

Was it two years ago that I'd noted the tide high in the pill, as it was now? "The salt water covered the Stepping Stones, and the trees of the woods along the bank washed their lower branches in it. Swans paddled there, unmoved, in their majesty, by the rattling and the rumbling on the railway. Mallard and moorhen seemed fussier – rising briefly from, then falling back on to, the surface", where the back-water "opened up" into the salt-estuary of Barn Lake. The better part of two years had passed. There had been war. There might be peace. Westfield Mill and the lower pill showed none of it. The peace, there, had been unbroken, and time might well have stood still.

At the station, my father – despite his "attacks" and looking paler, greyer, smaller – was waiting for me. At home, my mother greeted me. "Thank you, Boy", she said. "I'm glad ewe're home."

D'you know, I'm not certain that I was.

CHAPTER THIRTEEN

The Epilogue

Early in 1948, I received a letter from Principal Halliwell. I was living then as a lodger at 30 Frederick Street, Neyland. My parents had left 15 John Street and moved away. Bethesda Baptist Chapel had a new minister.

Despite my mother's appeal to me to give up thoughts of "foreign parts" and her gratitude on my returning to Neyland – where there was "so much" that I could do in the Sunday School, in the Band of Hope, in the Young People's Guild, to help Dad – my mother and I had under-estimated his dedication to his vocation. He had been "called" again. Unfit, physically, though he was, he had accepted the invitation of Carmel English Baptist Church, Aberdare, to be its pastor. My parents, to my mother's surprise, now lived at 32 Herbert Street, Foundry Town, in "sweet 'berdare".

Mam accepted the move with much-modified rapture and it left me stranded – a lodger, in limbo.

Before they'd left, they'd installed me, as a paying guest, in the home of Bethesda members Mr. Gilbert John and Mrs. Florrie John. It was home from home, but it wasn't my home. I was to lodge with them until Glenys and I were married – in Carmel, Aberdare – on 4th August, 1948.

It is, though, another couple's wedding that dates this epilogue for me. Glenys's sister, Mavis – our closest friend and confidante – had met and fallen in love with Danny Lester, who had been born in Hazelbeach, when he had returned to Pembrokeshire from five years of gruelling war service in North Africa and Italy.

Danny, serving with the R.A.F. Regiment, had played his part in actions to take and defend air-bases for the 8th Army in desert advances, and had done his bit in the subjugation of Italy, after the Messina landings. Some years older than I was – with much to tell, that he didn't, about the foreign service that had consumed his youth – he became a great friend. Ironic, sharply witty – his own man, in every way – he was to be a brother, rather than a brother-in-law, to me.

Mavis and Danny were married at Llanstadwell Church in the early morning of 30th March, 1948. Afterwards, the family lunched at the Mariner's Hotel at Haverfordwest. The bride and groom left for a London honeymoon. The Incledons lived at 35 High Street and, after seeing them safely returned there, I left them and crossed the ferry to Pembroke Dock. I had an evening date with my "almer mater". Trinity College was celebrating the centenary of its founding. Principal Halliwell's letter had invited me to join in.

There was a reason why I should begin my trip to Carmarthen at Pembroke Dock: in fact, there were several.

We were still in "austerity" Britain. In some ways, the first years of peace were shorter on supplies than the first years of the War had been. Petrol was still in short supply. Cars were difficult to obtain. It was easier to travel in groups, on hired coaches, or on the frequent trains.

Although I was, by then, teaching at Neyland County Primary School, where I had begun my own schooling twenty years earlier, my days at the Coronation School had strengthened my ties with "the Dock". You already know about the pool of Trinity College, Carmarthen, former students from the Pembroke area, active in teaching in South Pembrokeshire. A coach had been booked to take many of them to the Centenary Reunion Dinner. I'd been asked to join them as they took up the Principal's invitation to be a part of the celebrations.

There was then, of course, no bridge over the Cleddau. The last ferry-boat across the estuary left Hobb's Point at 9.30 p.m. I would have to stay in Pembroke Dock overnight when the coach returned. Cecil Parry's mother – though Cecil, fifty years later, denied it – had invited me to spend the post-dinner night at the Parrys' brand-new council-house, high on the hill in Pennar. While Cecil claims not to remember my being there, I can remember what we had for breakfast on the Sunday morning! Food was always important for me.

Soon after our contingent arrived at the College, Charlie Wilford dragooned all those wandering about – recapturing their lost youth between programmed events – into joining the Principal on the steps of the Broadcast Hall for an official photograph. Looking at that photograph now, I'm surprised by a number of things. Let me list them.

Some of those photographed would have had to make a fair long journey back into history to recapture any of the impulses of youth. The wing-collars and cravats of the Croats, of the "Black Prince", and of Queen Victoria's Consort, were pearl-pinned about their necks. Some ancients, some middle-aged, had their wives with them; more females than the College had hosted in its century. Some – especially among our Pembrokeshire group – wore no ties at all.

The fact that they didn't brings Principal R. C. White to mind yet again. Someone had appeared at a morning Chapel service to sing, tieless, with the choir. His fresh, well-ironed. white shirt-collar was spread out across his blazer revers. R. C. White took exception to his appearance. Barry Owen's lesson had not for him wholly been learned. "Why", he asked, "have you come to my choir dressed as a bus conductor?" Two conductors to one choir dismayed the man.

In the Centenary photograph, I am tieless. Nor am I, as I've said, the only one. Since we would, all of us, shortly be settling down for a formal dinner in the Examination Hall, the disparities in dress between casual and Victorian-dated seem surprising.

We might have had ties in our pockets, we open-throated ones. We would not, though, have had a change of clothing with us. Such times hadn't yet come for most of us. A recent, inaugural "dinner" of the South Pembrokeshire N.U.T. had convened in the upper-room of a chip-shop in Narberth and the "supper" had cost members half-a-crown – my pre-war wages for working Flossie Griffiths's cart around Neyland.

Many in the photograph would have been to a Chapel service and other gatherings earlier in the day. Some, with or without their wives, might well have occupied overnight rooms in the Wing. Whatever! Sports-coated, and flannelled, dark-suited and wing-collared, married and single, young and very old, eventually, we would sit down to dinner.

Before I report on that, let's spend a little more time on the group in the picture, and you are bound to be intrigued by the "back-drop" to the photograph. The "new, modern, Broadcast Hall" facade seems to have suffered from a war of its own! It certainly doesn't appear new or modern only a decade and a half after its opening. Perhaps we've forgotten now that so much of our environment had become shabby during the war, as all

Trinity College, Carmarthen, Centenary Reunion: 1848-1948.

resources were diverted to winning the victory. Curiously, the face of the Hall typifies the exhaustion – not simply of resources, but the near bankruptcy of Britain – when the total war was done. With three hundred thousand houses a year to be built, the faces of College buildings would have had no priority in that difficult time of recovery. Perhaps there had been a bit of Jerry-building, too, before "the Jerrys" began bombing Britain.

In front of that tired façade, one of the ladies sitting near – perhaps, next to – the Principal was not the oldest in the picture, but she was, in Trinity terms, historic. She was the daughter of one of the first twenty-two students to register at the South Wales and Monmouthshire Training College on its opening day in 1848.

I wish that I could identify her among the ladies. Too many years have gone by for me to remember which is she. I can easily identify Miss Francis, in her splendid hat. She's beside Charlie Wilford – as she often seemed to be – and smiling, regally, but I'm not even certain now that the unique guest of the Principal was named, as I think she was, Mrs. Harries. She was there, though, and she was in the front row. I was there, though not in that row, and the fact that we both were, on that day, makes me, for as long as I may live, part of an unbroken thread of contact down the one hundred and fifty years of Trinity's history. That lady had held the hand of her father. I shook her hand. Fanciful, isn't it? But I like the thought of it, don't you? In a vicarious way, that day, I shook hands with the whole of Trinity's history.

I'm in the fourth row from the front. Cecil Parry – though he denied ever having been there – is standing beside me. He is second and I am third in from the stage-left-hand-side of that fourth row back. Charlie Wilford had placed us there.

Not only had he readily identified us but he'd linked us with our years of attendance in an impressive feat of memory, even allowing for whatever swotting he might have done from the booking list. "Parry, 'Sam'", he'd shouted. "Parry, Cecil – '43, '45 – move over a bit!" He'd moved many others about like that, too.

Whatever else went on between the taking of the photograph and dinner, I was greeted, as we went into it, by Captain Ithel Thomas. "Parry", he said. "I want you to do the vote of thanks." Since Cecil still can't remember being there at all, and I tend to concentrate on remembering my own part in events, I can't tell you whether the Captain put us up in a revival of our occasional

'43-'45 double-act or not. In due course, though, I was called by the Master of Ceremonies. The great day was almost done. There was little that my vote of thanks to all concerned could add, but Pat O'Brien and the Plaza Cinema, Neyland, came to my aid, as they often did. I had seen him take over command of the Regiment and had his speech to the men by heart. He was conscious of the great history and fine traditions of that Regiment. He was humbled at having to walk in the footsteps of the mighty men who'd preceded him. His exit-words invited plagiarism as much as, and more than, his early ones. "We may not be able to add glory to that great history or to those fine traditions but we should pray that we never do anything to detract from them." At ten o'clock at night of a long day and after a good meal, almost half-a-century ago, you could get away with stealing other men's thunder and, as Abraham Lincoln said, "The World will little care nor long remember what we say ..."

There had been a series of real speeches, welcomes, greetings, identifications and presentations of the great and the good who had gathered.

Mrs. Harries was one of the speakers. She told us of her father's reminiscences about his time at the brand-new South Wales and Monmouthshire Training College. That's why I know that, on arrival, he and his colleagues filled the palliasses for their dormitory beds from a heap of dried rushes cut from the bogs. They'd been issued with a bill-hook, what's more, and told to cut down a quantity of green standing rushes and to spread them out to dry, replenishing the stock for later arrivals. It was, you remember, 1848.

In 1848, revolution ran riot on the continent of Europe. The French Republic was proclaimed. There were uprisings in Vienna, Bohemia and Hungary. In Germany, the Frankfurt Parliament convened. In Britain, the third Parliamentary Reform Bill was enacted.

The turbine engine was invented by Sir Charles Algernon Parsons, who also paced the genius of Isambard Kingdom Brunel by building the first turbine-driven steamship, making the remoter shores of the seven seas accessible to the gun-boats of the British Empire, as Marx and Engels produced the Communist Manifesto that was to become the Bible of Russia's secular imperialism. There was political pressure and rising radicalism in Britain, too, and, in that context, even modest claims for the extension of democracy at home sounded like sedition.

That year, the Chartists marched in thousands on Kennington Common. John Frost, Zephania Williams and William Jones – our Welsh demanders of democracy – were already serving out "life in transportation" and counting themselves lucky to have escaped hanging, drawing and quartering for their own march on Newport. Only the young Disraeli's influence on the younger Queen Victoria, I believe, prevented that. Eleven years earlier, still a teenager, she had succeeded to the British throne, and he, at thirty-three, had taken a seat in Parliament.

Why, I wonder, did he write, in his novel, "Coningsby": "Youth is a blunder; Manhood is a struggle; Old age is a regret"? Perhaps because of the pain of the anti-Semitism that he fought all his life and over which he seemed to have triumphed.

Modern students of Trinity might well shudder a bit to recall that, while plans for their College were being drawn, in January, 1840, their great-grandparents' generation – having the nerve to demand a say in the way they were governed and to march into town to say so – were lucky to get away with their lives.

By one of those extraordinary coincidences that enliven memories, Glenys – my wife of all these years – and I have stood among the ruins of that awful Port Arthur prison at the extreme tip, "Hell's Mouth", of Tasmania, as far away from Wales as most Welsh people could ever get, and tried to imagine how the fifty-six-year-old ex-Justice of the Peace and former Mayor of Newport must have felt as he stood, in chains and broad-arrowed, hessian, convict garb, on that savage shore, while Mrs. Harries's father and his young contemporaries took up residence in their purpose-built and shining-new college.

The 1840s were hard and, for many, cruel times. Men and women who cared about "the children of the poor in Wales" knew that education could change that. "You must educate, educate, educate", their slogan ran, "then you can legislate, legislate, legislate."

The Church of England and those whom it inspired in Wales knew what they were about when they built their new college, high on its green Carmarthen hill, to produce "religious, self-denying, earnest teachers, trained and prepared for the work of instruction".

Since its opening day, the South Wales and Monmouthshire Training College – emerging from the shell of its beginnings – has provided a flow of teachers to staff the schools of Britain. Many of those teachers were religious. Some would have been self-denying. Most would – at the beginning, at any rate – have been earnest. And they staffed not only the schools to which they were appointed but the churches, the chapels, the political parties, the clubs and councils and committees, the choirs and cultural societies, of our Welsh nation and those of neighbouring Britain, too. Who, now, could measure, the accumulative influence of this once "poor man's university" of Wales over its century and a half of metamorphoses. Trinity College, today, is de facto a true university in its own right. De jure recognition of that – as the lawyers say – can't be far away, can it?

What sort of world, I wonder, will Trinity students of the future serve? Training teachers is, today, only an important, single feature of their multi-facetted College. Teaching Welsh, teaching Welsh students – helping to preserve and to propagate the Welsh language and culture – combine into another. Providing management and masters of technology, cultivating the skills to serve the needs of the post-industrial Wales, are a vital part of its new dynamic.

Trinity students, though – male and female, these many years – come from almost everywhere, now, to study almost everything. Its very sophisticated student body is international. Their college is growing still, physically, across its grounds and, educationally, far beyond its original bounds. It caters for rich and poor alike, world-wide.

Its basic mission need scarcely change at all. Where there are rich, there are poor. There are poor in Wales in 1996. There are poor in Britain. Two-thirds of the people of the world are poorer still. Food, clothing, shelter and education are as essential to them as they have been to the poor throughout history.

Fifty years ago and a bit, I "went up" to Trinity. In a sense, I've never "gone down". True, I've lived almost the whole of my life in my lovely "down-below" land of Pembrokeshire, but in between times, I've travelled many, many thousands of miles, by land, sea and air. I've seen the wonders and the blunders of the world, the beauties and the uglinesses of many countries.

Now, I'm into my 71st year on earth, having had my 70th birthday since I wrote the first sentence of this book in the glorious summer of 1995. I'll make that first sentence of these memories of mine the last, too, shall I?

When Samuel Davies died, almost no-one outside of Neyland would have noticed, but his dying opened up the world for me.

Students contemporary with, and overlapping, the Alumnae of '43-'45

Abstracted from the not wholly reliable *College Year Book and Directory* published in 1948

1942-1944

Bray, R. W., West Ashling, Chichester, Sussex.
Burton, P. Gosport, Hants.
Buckthought, T.U., Troedyrhiw, Merthyr Tydfil.
Carter, 51 Parliament Street, Peterborough.
Checkley, C. M., Swansea.
Davies, B. A. F., Carmarthen.
Davies, E. J., Ammanford, Carms.
Davies, D. A. E. J., Bwlchnewydd, Blaenffos, Boncath, Pembs.
Davies, J. E. J., Brecon.
Davies, W. E., Merthyr Vale, Glam.
Davies, W. T., Rhondda, Glamorgan.
Eustis, J. V., Treboeth, Swansea.
Evans, G. R., 51 Mooring Road, Upper Tooting.
Evans, R. M., Pontypridd, Glam.
Evans, S. G., Llandyssul, Carms.
Evans, W. L., 119 Norman Avenue, Nuneaton, Warwickshire.
Eveleigh, R. S., Treorchy, Rhondda, Glam.
Finney, G., Blaina, Monmouthshire.
Fry, R. E., Shipston-on-Stour, Warwickshire.
Gill, R. J., Wallasey, Cheshire.
Gillett, M., Ventnor, Isle of Wight.
Gregory, J. D., Uppingham, Rutland.
Griffiths, D. T. O., Tregaron, Cards.
Grist, F., Manselton, Swansea.
Harvey, K. R., 2 High Fields, Great Dunmow, Essex.
James, R. A., Merthyr Tydfil.
Jenkins. D. S., 48 Lone Road, Clydach, Swansea.
Jones, R. D., Maerdy, Rhondda.
Jones, R. K., Cardigan.
Jones, S. H., Aberystwyth.
Jones, W., Pontyberem, Llanelly.
Lawrence, R. B., 105 Law Street, Pembroke Dock.
Lamont, F. C., 8 Margaret Street, Greenock, Renfrewshire.
Lee, W. A., 91 Rhyddings Terrace, Uplands, Swansea.
Meredith, E. E., Merthyr Tydfil, Glam.
Mordecai, G., Pontypridd.
Morris, J. L., Ystradgynlais, Swansea.
Nuttall, J., Rockdale.
Owen, H. E., Llanddarog, Carmarthen.
Porter, W. A., Dersingham, King's Lynn, Norfolk.
Price, J. I. O., Glenview, Solva, Pembs.
Richards, J. G,. Treboeth, Swansea.
Richards, N. D., Nantyglo, Brecon.
Roach, W. G. Aberayron, Cards.
Sebire, H. T., Wallasey, Cheshire.
Sheen, B. G. P., Abertillery, Mon.
Shepherd, D. C., Essex Home School, Chelmsford.
Sherratt, C. A., Cresswell, Stoke-on-Trent.

Tatchell, G. M., Bryncethin, Bridgend, Glam.
Thomas, J. A., Maesteg, Glamorgan.
Thomas, J. H., 108 Rectory Road, Grays, Essex.
Thomas, K. M., Pontypridd.
Thomas, W. H., Swansea.
Watkins, G. H., Graigwen, Pontypridd.
Watkins, H. L., Beeston, Nottingham.
Watson, R. M., Whitechapel, Near Preston.
Williams, D. T., Ammanford, Carms.
Williams, F. M., C.P. School, Llanginning, Carms.
Williams, I. V., 5 Poplar Street, Troedyrhiw, Merthyr Tydfil.
Williams, P., Sketty, Swansea.
Williams, W. E., 62 Caerphilly Road, Cardiff.
Woodbine, R., West Bromwich.
Wright, E. G., Ely, Cambs.

1943-1945

Bailey, W., 25 Llwynmadoc Street, Graigwen, Pontypridd, Glam.
Beresford, B., West Bromwich.
Bowen, R. C., 64 Ystrad Fawr, Bridgend, Glam.
Brown, J. I., Nant, Marl, Neath-road, Ystradgynlais, Brecs.
Burgess, D., Port Talbot, Glam.
Cherry, P., Guernsey, Channel Islands.
Cummings, J. C., Merthyr Tydfil, Glam.
Davies, D. H. G., Merthyr Tydfil, Glam.
Davies, Evan, Garnant, Carms.
Davies, J. A., Oldham, Lancs.
Davies, J. G., Merthyr Tydfil, Glam.
Edwards, D. W., Pontypridd, Glam.
Ellis, A., 125 Calton Road, Gloucester.
Evans, D. O., Aberayron, Cards.
Evans, John, Aberdare, Glam.
Evans, R. D., Bridgend, Glam.
Evans, R. P., 32 Holden Road, Wednesbury, Staffs.
Evans, T. P., Llanddarog, Carms.
Gravell, T. H., Kidwelly, Carms.
Griffiths, Alun, Carmarthen.
Harvey, H. E. Farnborough, Hants.
Hogarth, T. K., 2 Alexandra Terrace, Llantwit Fardre, Pontypridd.
Holder, F., Rhondda, Glam.
Hopkins, J. L. H., Oswestry.
Hughes, M. E., Aberfan, Glam.
Hughes, W. M., Bronwydd, Carms.
Jenkins, E.J., Bryn Awel, Tynmawr, Rumney, Cardiff.
Jones, J. G., Bridgend Inn, Pontyberem.
Lamborn, Eric, Port Talbot, Glam.
Lewis, T. N. N., Bryn Amlwg, Llanstephan, Carms.
Mayberry, W. J. D., Morriston. Glam.
Mayne, L. B., 11 Priory Street, Port Talbot, Glam.
Mills, S., Rossendale, Lancs.
Morgan, A. G., Abergavenny, Mon.
Morgan, M. L., Bridgend, Glam.
Morgan, William, 2 Upper Street, Maesteg, Glam.
Morris, B., Bridgend, Glam.
Moule, R. T., Clevedon, Somerset.
Noble, H., Brynmawr, Brecon.
Oliver, D. L., Aberystwyth.
Orsman, E. A. Lamphey, Pembs.
Owen, E. B., Narberth, Pembs.
Palmer, T. K., Stamford, Yorks.
Parry, C., Pembroke Dock.
Parry, G. S. D., "Wistoria," Promenade, Neyland, Pembs.
Peregrin, H., Penrhiwceiber, Glam.
Powell, L. M., 4 Beech Road, Oxley, Wolverhampton.
Preece, H. W., Abercrave, Swansea.
Ray, K. J. B., 24 Beech Drive, Hengoed, Glam.
Rees, C. G., Tonyrefail, Glam.
Rees, Graham, Ponthenry, Llanelly.
Rees, J. D., Newbridge, Mon.
Rhapps, T. M., 41 Lisbon Avenue, Twickenham, London.

Rowlands, D. T., 34 Thomas Street, Abertridwr, Caerphilly, Glam.
Stanford, A. G. D., Wokingham, Berks.
Thomas, D. W. T., Porthcawl, Glam.
Thomas, G. F., 29 Atherfold Road, Clapham, London.
Thomas, Iorwerth, Rhondda, Glam.
Thomas, T. L., Corner House, Tregaron, Cards.
Thomas, W. G., Ammanford, Carms.
Truran, L. H., Redruth, Cornwall.
Walker, W. G., Port Talbot, Glam.
Watkins, John, Blaina, Mon.
Watkins, Iorwerth, 7 Brynawel Road, Ystradgynlais, Swansea.
Watkins, Leslie, Amman Cottage, Glanamman.
Weeks, M. S., Ocean Police Station, Blaengarw, Glam.
Williams, D. B., 1 Penygarn Terrace, Maesteg, Glam.
Williams, D. G., Brynsiloh, Nanternis, Cards.

1944-1946

Abraham, D. D., 91 Cemetery Road, Porth.
Adams, T. E., Swansea.
Barnes, J. E., Wigan.
Bore, I. J., Blaina, Monmouthshire.
Bowen, I. H., Brynawel, Pwll, Llanelly.
Clayton, R. R., Pontypridd, Glam.
Coombe, W. D., Llanfoes, Brecon.
Davies. A. H. C., Rosedale, Bridge Street, Lampeter, Cards.
Davies, D., Penybont, Llanfynydd, Carms.
Davies, G., 97 Ropewalk Road, Llanelly.
Davies, H. C., 41 Brook Street, Taibach, Port Talbot.
Davies, I. J., Aberdare, Glam.
Davies, J. V. L., Wern Road, Skewen, Glam.
Davies, K. A., Lamphey, Pembs.
Davies, N. O., Bryn-Hedydd, Boncath, Pembrokeshire.
Davies, L. Gwys House, Upper Cwmtwrch, Swansea.
Davies, W. J., Llanddarog, Carms.
Donne, J. R. V., Glais, Swansea.
Edwards, D. P., High Street, Much Wenlock, Salop.
Evans, H. W., Post Office, Newchurch, Carmarthen.
Eustis, R., 2 Penlan Road, Treboeth, Swansea.
Hartingan, J. P., 155 Llangyfelach Street, Swansea.
Hoare, D. W. J., 18 Harefield Road, Brockley, S.E.4.
Hodges, J. R., Bridgend, Glam.
Hopkins, P. H., Ely, Cardiff.
Hughes, W. G., Treorchy, Rhondda.
Jeffreys, A. P., Tylorstown, Rhondda.
Jeffreys, W. D., Swansea.
Jenkins, D. L., Bronwydd Arms, Carmarthen.
John, T. G., Garnant.
Jones, D. D., 35 Windermere Ave., Roath Park, Cardiff.
Jones, D. H., Beaufort, Mon.
Jones, E. T., Cobridge Vicarage, Burslem, Stoke-on-Trent, Staffs.
Jones, Graham, 105 Lammas Street, Carmarthen.
Jones, G. G., 74 Adam's Avenue, Northampton.
Lawrence, W. J., Bryntaf, Backe, St. Clears.
Lewis, I. L., Ely, Cardiff.
Lewis, R., 139 Richmond Road, Cardiff.
Lewis, S. J. M., Nantyglo, Mon.
Malpass, J., Royston, Near Barnsley, Yorks.
Morgan, J. H., 9 College View, Llandovery.
Morgan, W. R., Porthcawl, Glam.
Morgans, J. H., The Bank, Llangendeirne, Kidwelly.
Morgan, H. A., 4 Hawthorne Terrace, Aberdare, Glam.
Nicholas, S. O., Llanelly.
Nancollas, H. J., Llanelly.

Parfitt, M. N., 135 Bonvilston Road, Pontypridd, Glam.
Pearce, W. E., Village House, Peterston, Ely, Cardiff.
Phillips, D. H. J., Llanelly.
Phillips, Kenneth, Carmarthen.
Pearce, G. J., Garndolbenmaen, Caernarvonshire.
Price, T. H. P., Aberdare.
Rees, A. E., Hunters Hall for Boys, Rockwell Road, Dagenham.
Short, A. J., Crickhowell, Brecon.
Thomas, R. G., 5 Alexandra Terrace, Mountain Ash, Glam.
Thomas, Ronald, Bryn House, Station Road, Ystradgynlais.
Tucker, T. I., Treboeth, Swansea.
Whittaker, S. J., Cherry Cottage, Goldcliffe, near Newport, Mon.
Williams, E. E., 10 Woodbine Terrace, Pembroke.
Williams, E. Ll., Crug Villa, Brecon.